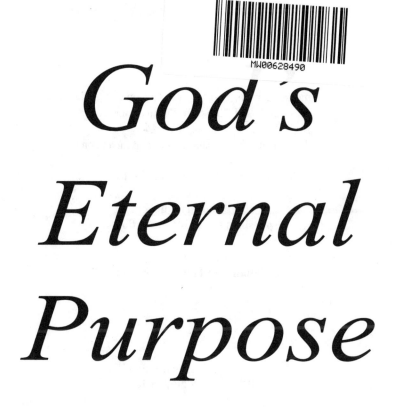

God's Eternal Purpose

The Making of Man in God's Image

by Dick York

The message in this book is available on CD, and can be
purchased from SOF Publications.

Also available by the same author in print and on CD

Truth or Tradition: Does it Matter?

**I Will Build My Church:
Ephesians for This Generation**

**Laws End:
Galatians for This Generation**

ISBN 978-1-889575-01-8

**SOF Publications
296 NE Alpenview Lane
Bend, Oregon 97701**

Phone: (541) 330-6684
E-mail: dickyork@dickyork.net

A Foreword

It would be an unhappy experience to be employed by someone and not know what you were to do. If you hadn't found out within the first forty hours you would probably quit or be fired. No one can function well if he doesn't know his purpose.

When it comes to life, however, some people exist for forty years, or even a whole lifetime without learning that they have been placed in this world for a purpose. They know neither their own purpose in particular, nor the purpose of mankind in general. Therefore, they invent a purpose of their own, which may seem worthwhile, and may provide a present challenge and temporal satisfaction, but ultimately, in eternity, will miss the mark. Proverbs 14:12 says, "There is a way that seemeth right unto a man, but the end thereof are the ways of death." Unfortunately, that "death" hangs as a pall over the whole race of unregenerate man.

Also unfortunate is the fact that within contemporary Christianity there is a segment that seeks to provide "biblical" principles for success in the pursuit of one's own agenda. this is an oxymoron, more humanistic than Christian. It contradicts the "cross" by which the flesh is crucified to make way for God's plan in the believer's life.

Biblical "separation" from the world has become an obsolete doctrine among many professing believers. Hence, the growing problem of which the apostle Paul forewarned us:

"Having a form of godliness, but denying the power thereof." (II Timothy 3:5). Biblical separation is the outcome of two things: 1) an ear to hear what the Spirit of God is saying, and 2) an understanding of what God's purpose is for humanity. It is the latter point I have attempted to deal with in this book.

As I preached about God's Eternal Purpose in various countries, I often heard the same question, "Is this message available in print?" The answer was, "No," because I had had no inclination to write. However, while teaching these foundational truths to workers in the church in Nigeria, I was impressed to write them down. This small book was the result. From that time, many have benefitted from it, and some have even used it as a tract to aid in evangelism. Some slight revisions have been made in this newest edition. Please read it and pass it on. I tust it will be a blessing to many.

Dick York

Bend, Oregon

2007

Contents

Chapter 1

Introduction to the Plan

Salvation is of The Lord

My friends and I had been warned often and sternly by the angry owner of the shingle mill to stay away from his pond. It was more like a floating corral than a pond. Long logs chained together kept the shingle bolts from floating away in the fast moving tidal current of Burrard Inlet in Western Canada. The treacherous current presented the danger of drowning if one of us should fall in the water. But, in spite of his warning, for 10-year-olds it was an exciting game to run across the flat shingle bolts.

We called them lily pads. They were 18 inch slices of cedar logs that would be split into shingles. None of them would support our weight. If we stopped on one it would sink or flip over, but if we moved fast enough from one to the next we could run all the way across the pond. Then, from the safety of one of the logs, we would look back over the bobbing lily pads we had set in motion.

On one occasion I decided to run back before they stopped bobbing. About the middle I made a misstep and slipped into the dark water under the cedar bolts. Struggling to surface I couldn't separate them enough to rise between them. Moreover, the relentless undercurrent was pulling me down. My lungs bursting, I realized in seconds I would inhale the salty water and drown.

Helpless to save myself, I had given up when suddenly something poked me hard between the shoulders. I was propelled forcibly upward between the lily pads by a pike pole hooked under the collar of my shirt. Soon I was standing on a log with my savior, the angry mill owner, telling me to leave and never come back. I was so thankful he had been willing and able to save me even though I had earned his displeasure by my performance.

My rescue had been entirely in his hands. I think of that incident often when I read in my Bible, "Salvation is of the Lord." But many seem unconvinced of that regarding their eternal soul. There are two problems in professing Christian circles which indicate that the understanding of God's purpose in the salvation process — and it is a process — is often obscure.

Problem 1: Salvation Depends On Performance

Even though their doctrine states otherwise, it is difficult for some Christians to escape the feeling that their salvation is somehow dependent upon good performance. There's a secret worry that, because they are unable to meet some self-imposed standard, God can't accept them. Most Christians know the Bible teaches that salvation is by grace[1] and not by any works of righteousness.[2] Nevertheless, many struggle with secret doubts when they take inventory of their performance record. It's evident that their confidence is in their works, but the idea of being saved by works cannot produce a changed life. That's the first problem, and it's more widespread than we might imagine.

Problem 2: Assurance Depends On Emotions

The second problem is the prevailing belief that assurance of salvation is a feeling one gets. Almost nobody teaches that, of course, but it's just the way many believers think. They are guided by emotion. After making an emotional decision they expect the resulting feeling to last forever. It doesn't, and they are disillusioned with their experience.

I John 5:13 says, ". . .these things are *written* that ye may know that ye have eternal life. . ." What God has promised he has put in a written contract which cannot change.[3] It is on that word that we are to base our confidence. But even knowing this, there are those whose confidence rises and falls with the tide of their emotions. This unfounded faith does not produce the lasting assurance, stability, or godliness which is the evidence of a saved life.

There are many examples of the consequence of these misunderstandings. Here is one.

Curtis seems to love God. He is outspoken about him in virtually any kind of company. He is uninhibited in his witnessing, loves to pray, and delights in the company of other believers. He says he was saved a few months ago and has all the enthusiasm of a new believer. On the other hand, he will tell you about being saved six years ago in prison; then of the terrible trouble he endured because of subsequent criminal behavior. Then he heard God's voice and was saved again three years ago while still in prison. He follows this with a story of being drunk on the street after his release and being led to the Lord by some street evangelists. Curtis' testimony leaves one wondering what he thinks salvation is. Unfortunately such testimonies are not unusual.

SOLUTION: Seeing From God's Perspective

There is a solution to these problems. It lies in a clear understanding of the gospel. Our salvation story did not begin with us. It was God's idea, and he is the author of it. Our salvation is not based on a decision we make, but in a work that he has done.

It is not uncommon when presenting the gospel, for a preacher to begin with the New Testament story of Jesus, and, after the briefest of explanations, to press the listeners to "make a decision." Many have been saved that way. So what's the problem?

The problem is that salvation is by believing. Decisions are made with the head. They may or may not be the result of believing. That's why multitudes who make decisions may not be saved. Believing is a heart conviction that may not even remotely resemble an act of decision making. Often people are asked to make decisions when they have not yet been provided with the information they need to believe. Decisions without faith may produce an emotional moment, but they won't produce salvation. Genuine faith, on the other hand, brings salvation, and a new life, even without a conscious

9

act of deciding.

The Whole Word of God

If you will hold between the thumb and index finger of your left hand all the pages of the Old Testament (Genesis to Malachi), and between the thumb and index finger of your right hand all the pages of the New Testament (Matthew to the Revelation), you may be surprised as you compare the thickness of the two. The Old Testament is more than three times the size of the New. Yet all of those pages are often treated as though they are not important to the gospel message.

What is all that stuff you are holding in your left hand? That is the foundation of all that you are to believe about the New Testament. Faith comes by hearing, and hearing by the whole Word of God.

Because it is God's story, and because he has told it to us precisely and in detail, we are to believe it as he has said it. In John 7:38 Jesus stated, "He that believeth on me *as the scripture hath said*, out of his belly shall flow rivers of living water."

We may interpret this to mean that somewhere in the scriptures (meaning the Old Testament) it is stated that if you believe on Jesus, out of your belly will flow living water; and Jesus is apparently quoting from that passage. But, that is not the case. There is no such verse in the Old Testament.

What Jesus is saying is that he that believes on him the way the scriptures instruct him to believe—ie: believe what the scriptures say about Jesus: who he is, why he would come, how he would be born and where, and the myriad prophecies that foreshadow his coming, trusting implicitly in him as the coming savior they describe—then, out of that believers belly will flow rivers of living water.

Obviously, someone who is a comparative stranger to the Bible doesn't understand initially all that is in it; but to trust Jesus as Lord and Savior we need to know the basics of what the Bible says about him. The information we need to base our faith upon is about him, not about us.

The foundations of the gospel message begin in Genesis 1:1 with God creating the heaven and the earth, and continue from there to explain the marvelous truths that we will trust if we are believers: creation, the beginnings of everything, the fall and its ramifications, etc. The whole Old Testament is a progressive revelation of the saviour who was promised to reconcile Adam's fallen race to God. We are to believe the unfolding of truth that finally brings us to Jesus in the New Testament. All of this is the Word of God, given to us to lay foundations for our faith.

There are many kinds of faith, but there is only one kind that saves. Biblical faith is based on God's revealed truth. It rests on the eternal promises that God has made throughout his Word and which he cannot fail to keep. Simply put, *faith is trusting God*.

Trusting God involves confidence in his character. We must be able to trust what he says. The New Testament assures us that "God *cannot* lie."[4] In the book of Hebrews we read that "it is *impossible* for God to lie."[5] It is not merely that God *won't* lie, It is that he *cannot* lie. It is not even a remote possibility. It is entirely outside of God's character to lie. That is the first foundation of biblical faith. We can believe what he says.

Secondly, God, who cannot lie, has made certain immutable promises. Obviously, if God had never said anything, regardless of his impeccable character, there would be nothing for us to believe. But he has said something, and because he cannot lie, his promises cannot fail. That is the second foundation of Biblical faith. It is confidence in the immutable promises of a God whose perfect character precludes even the remotest possibility of falsehood or failure.

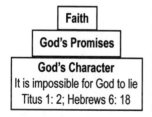

Our faith rests firmly on the promises of the God who cannot lie. That is the firm foundation of faith; not our feelings, our emotions, our performance, nor our human reasoning.

The record God has given us in the Bible is a chronological revelation of his character, his plan and his ultimate eternal purpose.

11

It begins at the beginning, and takes us beyond the end of time. God's purposes are eternal, his planning is precise, and his ways are perfect. The result for us will be perfection.

Unbelieving men, watching history unfold with its famines, wars, human suffering, and injustice, have concluded that if, indeed, there is a God, he is capricious. Perhaps he is even sadistic, as he watches apathetically the agony of his suffering creation. But those who believe see in the unfolding of history an amazing precision that testifies to the absoluteness of God's truth.

There is a sense in which God has not finished his work. Making man in his image began with Adam but will be finished when we see Christ. It is essential we understand that conforming created man to the image of the eternal God is a continuing process.[6] To see what God is doing and why he is doing it is to gain a confidence, a stability, and a singleness of eye for which many of us have longed. Even more than seeing the process, we must see the God behind the process. All things were created by him and for him,[7] therefore he is central to everything that exists. When we understand that, and commit ourselves to him, we experience his life changing salvation. Otherwise man is frustrated by his own inadequacy to live as he thinks would please God.

Let's put this in perspective.

GOD: Who Is He?

We are whizzing through space at over seventeen thousand miles per hour on a ball revolving at one thousand miles an hour, yet we are not conscious of speed or of the tremendous energy being expended. Somehow centrifugal force does not catapult us into space, nor do we have any sensation of motion at all. On the contrary, we gaze into the tranquil night sky bedecked with countless shining jewels stuck on a velvet ceiling that seems to belong exclusively to the earth. We, it seems, are the center of the universe.

There are over five billion "centers of the universe" on this earth, each pursuing his own agenda. Perhaps only a fraction of our number recognizes the personality who has placed the universe in motion and presides over it all.[8] It is possible that most of us lack an accurate concept of the creator. Even we who acknowledge him frequently relegate him to that oft-neglected segment of our life-style we call our "religion," thus he neither hinders nor enhances our personal agenda.

There are those who seem excited about what God could potentially do for them. They sit at the feet of those who teach formulas which will, supposedly, tap into something called "the power of God." This will enable *them* to accomplish *their* will, improve *their* health, increase *their* wealth, or stimulate *their* business.

In this concept man is the center, and God exists to help him. This is a form of humanism. When things go man's way he may say, "Praise God." When they don't he frets. Too few, perhaps, see God as he really is — the ultimate authority for whose purpose all things exist.

Too little is understood about the person of God and the purpose behind his dealings with man. Yet, in order to walk joyfully and at peace in all our circumstances we need to understand what God's eternal purpose is. To do that we need to understand something of God's person.

Perhaps it is because of the lack of insight into his person that people do not seek God for himself. In John 4 the story is told of Jesus confronting the Samaritan woman at the well of Sychar. He asked her for a drink. She was immediately suspicious of his motives and responded, "How is it that you, being a Jew, ask drink of me, a woman of Samaria? for Jews have no dealings with Samaritans."

Jesus answered, "If you knew the gift of God, and who it is that said unto you, Give me to drink; you would have asked of him, and he would have given you Living Water."

If you knew two things, Jesus said, you would have asked. Those two things are 1. The gift of God and 2. Who Jesus is. People do not seek him, because they know neither the gift of God, nor who he is.

The psalmist David knew who God was. He recognized his fingerprints on the creation. He wrote, "The heavens declare the glory of God, and the firmament shows his handiwork."[9] The heavens are not the glory of God; they simply declare it. The firmament is not the sum total of his handiwork, but an evidence of it. As awe inspiring as the heavens are, David knew God is greater than his handiwork, even as "he that builds the house is greater than the house."[10] Jesus came to reveal the Father. All that he said declared God's greatness, and all that he did revealed his character. Even in what we call 'the Lord's Prayer,'[11] Jesus gives us glimpses of the greatness and majesty of the Father.

"Thine is the Kingdom."[12] Jesus said the Kingdom of Heaven belongs to God. He reigns over it. There are men who have had glimpses into that kingdom: Daniel, Ezekiel, John, Paul, and others. Dumbfounded, they could not describe its glory. Some of them fell on their faces as dead men, overcome with awe. Even so, the combined total of all they saw did not reveal the kingdom of God. "Eye has not seen, nor ear heard, neither have entered into the heart of man the things which God has prepared for them that love him."[13] There is infinitely more than has been seen or even imagined. Yet God is greater than all the kingdom over which he reigns.

"And the Power." Jesus added that all power belongs to God. We have a small insight into power. The law of thermodynamics teaches us that neither energy nor matter can be created or destroyed, only converted from one state to the other.[14] Whatever power there is, has existed from the beginning. Man has learned how to convert mass to energy but still struggles with the dream of converting energy to mass. That power still belongs to God alone. Even if it were within man's ability, it would require all the energy consumed by the city of Chicago for one whole year to produce a single pound of matter.[15]

The earth comprises 6.587×10 to the 21st power tons of mass, or 13,170,000,000,000,000, 000,000,000 pounds.[16] In other words, it would require all the energy consumed in Chicago for 13 septillion, 170 sextillion years to produce matter equivalent to the earth's mass. Yet the earth is only a minuscule particle of the universe.

The energy that brought, not only the earth, but all the galaxies into being is immeasurable. That power is identified in the scriptures as the 'Word of God.' *"By the Word of the Lord were the heavens made; and all the host of them by the breath of his mouth. ....Let all the earth fear the Lord: let all the inhabitants of the world stand in awe of him. For he spoke and it was done; he commanded, and it stood fast"* (Psalm 33:6, 8, 9)

Furthermore, the power that holds all things together and keeps us from spinning off the earth — indeed, keeps every atom from disintegrating from centrifugal force — is that same 'word of his power.'[17]

"And the Glory." It is his, Jesus said. The glory of God is incomparable. Moses, who stood in the glory cloud on Mt. Sinai for forty days literally shined. He had to cover his face with a veil because the people could not bear to look upon the glory he had absorbed in God's presence.[18] So brilliant is God's glory, the scriptures teach us, that the enemies of God in the time of his judgement will be consumed with the brightness of his presence.[19]

In this age of travel many of us have been privileged to see the spectacular beauty of this planet: from the Grand Tetons in Wyoming to the Canadian Rockies; the grandeur of the Swiss Alps to the towering Himalayas; the craggy fjords of Norway and the spectacular coasts of New Zealand. I sat one day before a giant Imax screen and watched amazing shots of "the blue planet" earth, taken from an orbiting space shuttle. I marvelled at God's creation as I saw our planet floating like an opal over a background of black velvet.

On another occasion, while travelling alone through the Canadian Rockies, I found the beauty so distracting I was compelled to stop my car. What a tribute, I thought, to the divine skill of the creator. If one could behold at one time all the beauty of the earth, with every blazing sunset, the spectacle of every coral reef with its symphony of colors, the breathtaking view from every mountain top, the sight would only hint at God's glorious majesty. Amazingly, it is God's desire to reveal this glory to his people. In fact, it was for this very reason that God Created humanity, that we might one day praise his glory.

As I stood beside my car drinking in the beauty of my surroundings, I wished my wife and family were there to share it with me. I'm sure I am not the only one who has desired to share some great pleasure with someone else. After all, that's what makes our enjoyment complete. That fact illustrates for us God's eternal purpose.

It was God's divine pleasure to reveal his majestic glory to many sons. It will one day be God's delight to see the joy on the immortal faces of his translated sons as they are astounded by the splendor of his glory. Their inexpressible joy will cause them to burst forth in spontaneous, eternal praise. And God who created, predestined, adopted, and redeemed his people specifically for that purpose — to praise his glory[20] — will be pleased.

Some, who measure God as they would man, may find fault with his desire to be praised. "That," they might say, "is the height of egoism." In a man that would be true. No man has the right to self-adulation. God, however, has the right to be exalted. He is before all things. By him all things consist.[21] His name, YHWH (Yahweh, Yehowah [Jehovah]) means *The Eternally Existing One.* Redeemed people will one day sing, "Thou art worthy, O Lord, to receive Glory and honor and power, for thou has created all things, and for thy pleasure they are and were created."[22]

God's redeemed ones will one day understand that. In fact, they should understand that now. All things, including us, were made for him. We are to please him, not he us. The Psalmist wrote, "It is God who has made us and not we ourselves."[23] God made us *for himself.* When we see that, we will happily submit to him, even as Job, who said, "Though he slay me, yet shall I trust in him."[24]

HUMANITY: Who Are We?

God desires the fellowship of his people. Throughout the scriptures he reveals his heart. Jesus, speaking for the Father, stood before Jerusalem and said, "O Jerusalem, Jerusalem, . . . how often would I have gathered thy children together even as a hen gathereth her chickens under her wings, and ye would not."[25]

We hear the Father's heart in that statement. Jesus revealed it again in the short parable in Matthew 13:44. "The kingdom of heaven is like unto treasure hid in a field; the which when a man hath found, he hideth, and for joy thereof goeth and selleth all that he hath and buyeth that field." The field is the world. The treasure is the elect people of God who make up the kingdom of heaven, but initially are lost in the world. The man is the Lord Jesus who has come forth from the bosom of the Father to procure that treasure.

The purchase price is "all that he had," his very life-blood, given to reconcile the world unto himself. God has made it clear that his greatest purpose is fellowship with his redeemed ones.

It's a mystery why God needs, or even wants, to fellowship with man. Even David, in one of his psalms asks, "What is man that thou art mindful of him?"[26] It makes little sense until we consider why God created man.

The average person readily confesses he does not know why God made man. Many have never thought about it. But we can be sure God thinks about it continually. After all, he made us for himself. But man, oblivious to that fact, in his fallen state tends to create a god in his own image who will serve his own purposes. It cannot be taken for granted that man has intuitively an accurate concept of God. He does not.

The world is filled with religious contradictions about God and millions of images that supposedly represent him. Only in the Bible do we have an accurate and authoritative description of God. Man's role is related to, and made understandable in, the light of what God is.

Jesus said, "God is a Spirit."[27] After his resurrection Jesus told his bewildered disciples, "A spirit hath not flesh and bones as ye see me have."[28] The apostle Paul, instructing Timothy, described God as eternal, immortal, and invisible.[29] The Psalmist David devoted an entire psalm[30] to extolling God's omniscience and his omnipresence. God is therefore described in the Bible as an invisible, omnipresent Spirit who is without flesh and bone. He is omniscient (knowing all things intuitively) and with all power and authority in heaven and earth. That comes as no surprise, of course, to any who have read their Bibles. But it may surprise some that that truth about God has everything to do with the purpose of man.

God existed, obviously, before any of his creation.[31] Filled with the marvelous glory we feebly attempted to describe earlier, he was (and is) also filled with all the attributes we know in man: love, compassion, mercy, patience, wisdom, even anger, etc. These appear in man because they are attributes of God, in whose image man was created.

Consider for a moment that each of these qualities, in order to

17

be fulfilled, requires expression. Love, for example, is manifested through giving. We are even admonished by the apostle John to "love not in word, but in deed and truth."[32] Love requires action, and giving is the action that expresses love. "God so *loved* the world that he *gave* his only begotten Son."[33] But giving requires a receiver as well as a giver. There must be an object of love. The same is true of compassion and mercy. Compassion, to be expressed, requires human need. Mercy is expressed in the light of human failure. Humanity, therefore, exists so that God's attributes may be expressed and his glory revealed.

Creation wasn't whimsical on God's part. He didn't wake up one Friday morning and say, "Let's see. What shall I do today? Maybe I should create something. Perhaps I will invent a man." On the contrary, God needed humanity; not in the sense that he would be in jeopardy without it but in the sense that humanity was necessary to the fulfillment of his plan.

Apart from humanity there would be no "image" of God. There would be none to whom God could express himself; no recipients of his love; no objects of his mercy. And, as has been stated, his attributes, to be manifest, must be expressed. Furthermore, without humanity there would be no sons to praise his glory.

But humanity was to be more than merely the object of God's expressed attributes. It was also to be the vehicle *through* which the invisible God would express himself.

Consider yourself for a moment. You are a triune being. The Bible makes it clear that you are spirit, soul and body. However, your image, that which is visible, is your body. I can't see your spirit or your soul, and yet it's there that all the emotions, the wisdom, the deliberations that make up your personality and character reside. It's there that conclusions are reached that generate the commands that cause your body to respond. And it is that response that others see and use to understand what is in your spirit.

I know when you love me by the look on your face and the things that you do and say in response to me. I know when you are angry with me by the scowl on your countenance. In other words, everything in your invisible being is expressed by your body, and always those expressions are directed at another person. If there were no other person they would be meaningless. That is what humanity is all about. It was to be the body through which, and to whom, the invisible God would express his character and reveal himself.

We can see this truth in the person of Jesus. He is the measure of perfect manhood, the man God meant all men to be. The Bible says, "No man has seen God at any time, but the only begotten son, (Jesus) who is in the bosom of the Father, he has declared (fully revealed) him.[34] Jesus is the one we will be like at the conclusion of it all.[35] He is the express image of the invisible God.[36]

God's Plan

The Bible is the revelation of God's eternal purpose. Two aspects of it are evident. The eternal aspect is only dimly revealed in the last two chapters of the Bible. The details are reserved for that day when we shall see him and know him even as we are known.[37] The other is the temporal aspect, the time-related process in which we are now involved, the fashioning of man in the image of God. It is through those who will be conformed to his image that God will work and reveal himself for all eternity. This temporal aspect of God's eternal plan involved the creation, the temptation, the fall, and the redemption of mankind.

There are those who would suggest a different view of history, one in which God created Adam in his own image as the finished product. Then, taking God by surprise, Satan slipped in and tempted Adam, causing him to fall. God then devised a remedial program of redemption to restore man to what he had been before the fall.

This may be a common perspective but not a biblical one. If this scenario were true, we would have reason for uncertainty concerning our eternal destiny. After all, if God lost the first round, how could we be absolutely sure he would not lose the last one also? This concept fails to recognize the sovereignty of almighty God who does all things after the counsel of his own will.[38]

Even Satan serves God, albeit unwillingly. His rebellion against God, his malevolence against the church, and his raging against righteousness, work to produce the circumstances and the trials that perfect the faith of the saints, and that conform them to the image of Christ.[39]

19

CHAPTER 1 References.

1. Ephesians 2:8
2. Titus 3:5
3. Psalm 119:89
4. Titus 1:2
5. Hebrews 6:18
6. Ephesians 4:12-14
7. Colossians 1:16
8. Psalm 33:6-9
9. Psalm 19:1
10. Hebrewa 3:3
11. Matthew 6:9-13
12. Matthew 6:13
13. I Corinthians 2:9
14. 2nd Law of Thermodynamics
15. Dr. Geo. Speak; Moody Science Institute
16. Calculus Text Book
17. Hebrews 1:3
18. Exodus 34; II Corinthians 3:7,13
19. II Thesselonians 2:8
20. . Ephesians 1:6,12,14
21. Colossians 1:17
22. Revelation 4:11
23. Psalm 100:3
24. Job 13:15
25. Matthew 23:37
26. Psalm 8:4
27. John 4:24
28. Luke 24:39
29. I Timothy 1:17
30. Psalm 139
31. Colossians 1:17
32. I John 3:18
33. John 3:16
34. John 1:18
35. I John 3:1,2
    Rom.8:28,29
36. Hebrews 1:3
37. I Corinthians 13:12
38. Ephesians 1:11
39. Romans 8:28

Chapter 2
The First Man

The Only Authorized Image

Undoubtedly, the most profound statement ever made concerning the visible, material order is, "In the beginning God created the heaven and the earth."[1] It says that God is, that he existed before the beginning, and that all things began through an act of creation by him. The Bible says all that in only ten words.

Like a bird preparing a nest for its young, God created the earth to be inhabited[2] by the man he had in mind before the world began. But before he created the man or anything else, he prepared a host of heavenly attendants to serve him. After preparing these angelic servants and an environment impeccably suited for human existence, God said, "Let us make man in our image."[3] In that moment the first and only authorized image of God was created. God has commanded in his Word that no other image should be made to represent him.[4] Man is the image of God.

When God said, "Let us make man in our image," however, he was looking beyond Adam, through the course of this world's history and beyond to another man, a man who conforms in every respect to the image of the eternal God. He was seeing the resurrected Christ and all who are in him. Adam was not the finished work but the beginning, and all the history of Adam's race is part of the process of making man in the image of God.

God created only one man. Every human body that has ever inhabited the earth was created in Adam's loins. Even the physical body of Jesus Christ came through Mary, a descendant of Adam.[5]

Though we may accurately say man was created in the image of God, the converse is not true. God is an invisible, omnipresent Spirit without flesh and bone. It is wrong therefore, to say, as some do, that God has the appearance of a man. God, according to the Bible, is invisible. Man was to be the image of the invisible God, and insofar as God's perfect will was demonstrated in his body before the fall, Adam was the image of God.

Man is a spiritual being as well as soul and body.[6] Originally, Adam was able to fellowship "spirit to Spirit" with God and, with no agenda of his own, yielded his body to be led by the Spirit of God. Had it been possible to observe Adam prior to the fall, one would have seen a perfect demonstration of what God was doing, in the actions of the man.[7]

That Adam was not the finished work is evident, because he could do two things that God could not. It is absolutely impossible for God to sin or to die. Adam, on the other hand, was created with the potential for both. We'll call that PSD (Potential of Sin and Death).

Why Is There Sin?

We have probably all heard the question asked, "If God is wise and omnipotent, why didn't he create Adam the way he wanted him to be? Why the potential to sin?"

It is because of his wisdom that he has done what he has done. His ways are higher than our ways, and his thoughts than our thoughts.[8] We, who now see in a glass darkly,[9] anticipate with joy that day when we shall see him face to face, when we will know him even as he knows us. Then we will understand his wisdom. In the meantime, the Bible is his revelation and through it we are able to gain some insights into his remarkable plan. We know from the scriptures that God sits in the heavens and does whatsoever he pleases.[10] "He works all things after the counsel of his own will."[11]

We know that there is sin and that it has infected the entire human race. Our newspapers, radios and televisions testify to that fact every single day. It doesn't come as a surprise when we read in the Bible that "all have sinned and come short of the glory of God."

The question persists. If the invisible God created man to be his image, and if sin is the factor that frustrates that purpose, causing man to be eternally separated from God, why did an omnipotent God allow sin in his creation? In fact, if nothing exists that God did not create, God himself must be responsible for the existence of sin in his creation.

God has filled his Bible with little windows that open onto the vast panorama of his truth. Three of these windows reveal the origin of sin, and this revelation defines what sin is, throwing light on the questions at hand.

The first window is Isaiah 45:7, *"I form the light, and create darkness: I make peace and create evil: I the Lord do all these things."*

We know that somehow evil was incorporated into the creation. We see it, of course, on every hand. Calamity, a synonym for the word "evil" that is used in several Bible translations, could describe the devastation caused by the 1993 hurricane that destroyed the south Florida coast, the disastrous mid-west floods that followed, or hurricane Katrina that destroyed the city of New Orleans on August 29, 2005. Or it could describe the havoc wrought upon a life through the consequences of sin.

God is the regulator of all that transpires in his creation. He is the creator of evil inasmuch as he is the creator of the evil one. This is not to suggest that God is the perpetrator of wickedness, but if he created the evil one and allows evil to exist in the world he created, it obviously has a function in his great plan.

The second window is Hebrews 1:14. The subject is the angels. Of them the writer says, *"Are they not all ministering spirits, sent forth to minister for those who shall be heirs of salvation?"*

This host of spirit beings, sent forth into the creation to serve those who would be saved, were created long before there were any saved people. They were brought into being, in fact, before there were any lost people. They existed before man was created. We can conclude, therefore, that salvation (redemption from sin) was in the mind of God before there was a sinner, indeed, before there was a human being. It is evident, then, that for some divine reason, redeemed man, specifically, is the object of God's whole program.

The third window, Ezekiel 28:12-15, reveals the personal history of the evil one, the angel Lucifer, by whom sin was introduced into the creation. Although he is described here as 'The King of Tyrus', the context makes it clear that he is a cherub (an angel) and that he has stood where no human being has been privileged to stand. *"Thou hast been in Eden, the garden of God. . .Thou art the anointed cherub that covereth . . . thou wast upon the holy mountain of God: thou hast walked up and down in the midst of the stones of fire."*

This angelic being was full of wisdom and perfect in beauty. There is little doubt that he is the same one who appears as a serpent in the garden of Eden. Beside Adam, Eve and God, the serpent is the only other character in that scene.

"Thou wast perfect in thy ways from the day that thou wast created, till iniquity was found in thee."

Iniquity had its origin in this angelic being, described elsewhere as Lucifer, the angel of light. We have already seen in Hebrews 1:14 that **all** the angels were sent forth to serve those who would be saved. *All*, obviously, would include Lucifer. We know also that those who will be saved are those who are to be the image of the invisible God. We know that Satan is an angel and that he is also an obvious enemy of righteousness, and unquestionably in violent rebellion against God. How then, we may well ask, can he be considered a servant of the saved ones? Obviously, he is not a willing servant, but even his rebellion cannot frustrate the purposes of God for him, and whatever he does to destroy God's plan ultimately contributes to its conclusion.[12]

Isaiah the prophet sees in the fall of Babylon a reflection of Lucifer's rebellion. In Isaiah 14:12-15 he gives us some insight into what the iniquity was, to which we referred earlier.

"Thou hast said in thine heart, I will ascend into heaven. I will exalt my throne above the stars of God; I will sit upon the mount of the congregation in the sides of the north; I will ascend above the heights of the clouds; I will be like the Most High."
Five times Lucifer expressed **his will**. Clearly it was not to be a servant of God but an equal; not a servant of man either, but an authority over him. The bottom line was, *"I will be like the Most High."*
"Most" is a superlative. "Most" cannot be exceeded nor equaled. There can be only one Most High. To be like him, or equal to him, would negate his superlative uniqueness and his singular authority. All absolutes which result from the supreme authority of the Most High would dissolve. It is this philosophy that challenges every principle of God's Word concerning science, law, moral values, marriage, etc. When one shuns God's authority and makes one's own rules, one is saying, in effect, "I will be like the Most High." This is the philosophy of sin.

When iniquity was found in Lucifer, God did not expel him to Pluto or Uranus, light years from the presence of man. On the contrary, he cast him down to the earth where he confronted Adam and Eve in their first home, the garden of Eden.[13] Sin, then, existed in the earth from the time that Lucifer was cast down, before man was ever created. Its presence created an antagonist to the expressed will of God for man. Without this presence, man would have simply served God without choice. Without the options it provided, there could have been no exercise of will, no god-likeness, no love, no obedience, no manifestation of faith, in short, no image of God.

All of the preceding attributes require options. It is unlikely one would be recognized as obedient if there were no option to be disobedient. Several years ago I worked with a man who would bring his beautiful golden retriever to the job site in the back of his pickup. He would tell the dog to stay, and nothing could coax that dog to jump out of the truck until his owner told him to. We would all marvel at the dog's obedience. I, on the other hand, once had a dog that had to be tied to a post to keep him in the yard. If he was commanded to stay he did it only because the rope frustrated his eager efforts to disobey. Staying in the yard against his will only because he had no other option could not be defined as obedience. Obedience requires the option of disobedience.

Faith, or trust, in like manner, requires the option of unbelief. During the days of the cold war, when many American troops were stationed in Europe and military exercises were the order of the day, a young soldier earned the admiration of some and the derision of many. It seems he was posted at a rural intersection in the country-side of West Germany. His orders were to remain there until he was picked up. The operation ended, but for three days no one came to pick him up. As he faithfully stood at his post for those three days and nights, the local people brought him food and water. Some of them urged him to leave and make his way back to his outfit. He replied that his orders were to stay put until he was picked up. Because he knew his rank and trusted his commander, he remained at his post until he was sent for. Although he was ridiculed by some of his peers, he was commended by his commander for obeying orders. His option, of course, was to consider his commander unworthy of trust and therefore create his own agenda.

The commander's trustworthiness in this case may have been questionable, but not so God's. Trust is only evident when circumstances or antagonists challenge it. The options of disobedience, hate, unfaithfulness, etc. exist in the world because of Satan's iniquity. When God cast him down to the earth the stage was set. All the ingredients for sin and all the options of choice were in existence from that time, before man was placed upon the earth.

The Stage Is Set

God created *all* things (including man) for his good pleasure.[14]

"Scientists" like to tell us that man has descended—or rather ascended—from lower life forms. The contrived evidence for such a theory is shaky and circumstantial at best. The most reliable evidence would indicate that man is created quite distinct from the rest of nature.[15] It is realistic to believe that Adam was the perfect specimen of manhood. He was the prototype of man. All who would come after may bear imperfections resulting from the sins and misbehavior of those who preceded them. But it is unthinkable that Adam, who was the direct product of God's hand would be less than perfect. And so he remained for a time unblemished by the consequences of sin.

As God is a triune being, he created the man to be a triune being also: spirit, soul, and body. But whereas God is invisible and omnipresent, the man was a visible being, made to be the visible image of the invisible God.

As well as being made in the *image* of God, man was made also in his *likeness*.[16] Because man's fall comes so early in the historical narrative, we have little opportunity to see much God-likeness in the human race. However, there are glimpses of this quality in the great men of faith whose names and stories are told in the Old and New Testaments. In the New Testament we read of the consequences of spiritual rebirth, the redemptive process that brings fallen sinners of Adam's race back into a right relationship with God and transforms them from the inside out.[17] Three of these consequent traits give us some insight into the "likeness of God."

The first is in Colossians 3:10. ". . .the new man. . .is renewed in **knowledge** after the image of him who created him."

To one who has struggled through years of college or some other form of study, knowledge is academic. Or to another who has learned through long years of apprenticeship or hard-earned experience, it may be technical. In either case it is attained through great effort and expenditure of time.

But there is another kind of knowledge. It is intuitive—the kind God has. He knows all things, not because he has studied all things but because he is the source of all things. We know how much rain fell in our city last year because we measured it. God knew intuitively. Adam was created with knowledge. Because he was an instrument and vessel of God, God's intuitive knowledge was available to him. In a limited sense this is true of those who have been redeemed and walk in the Spirit of God. They have access to the intuitive knowledge of God.[18]

That does not eliminate the need to acquire academic knowledge, but is itself a knowledge that cannot be attained through academics. Whereas fallen humanity must be renewed in this knowledge, Adam was created with it.

The second is Ephesians 2:10. *"We are his [God's] workmanship, created in Christ Jesus unto **good works**, which God has before ordained that we should walk in them."* Most of us are well aware of things about which we are ashamed or disappointed or at least that we would do differently if we had the opportunity. That's why there are jokes about New Year's resolutions every year. Before Adam's fall there was no such dilemma. Adam was created by God for a purpose, and his works were God's works. Just as Jesus Christ was later to say, "I do always the things that please him [God]."[19] Before the fall, that agenda for Adam was automatic. There was no other agenda. His works were exactly what God was inspiring him to do. In those works he was like God because they were the works of God. In our case, regeneration is God's re-creation of us. Ultimately we will have no other agenda but his.[20]

The third is Ephesians 4:23,24. *". . .be renewed in the spirit of your mind. . .put on the new man which after God is created in **righteousness and true holiness.**"* This describes God's will for man, who is to be his visible image. Adam bore this likeness.

In Adam's case, many would question the accuracy of describing him as "righteous" because righteousness is defined by its relationship to unrighteousness, just as obedience only exists in contrast to disobedience. In Adam's case many would rather call his right-doing "innocence." There is no quarrel with that. But still, righteousness is "doing right." It is action that reflects the perfect will of God.

True holiness is also a reflection of what God is. Holiness means to be set apart from all else, as God is distinct from his creation. He is holy. He is unchanged by everything around him because he is separate from it. In like manner, Adam was set in the earth, not merely as part of the creation but *over* it all [21] and distinct from the world of animals and plants. He was set over the works of God's hands. In relation to all of creation, he was holy. He was in the likeness of God.

We have already discussed the two factors that make us realize Adam was not the finished product, the ultimate man in the image of God. You will remember the term PSD to which you were introduced earlier. It is evident that God has no potential of sin or death, but Adam was created with both. He could sin, and if he did, he was told he would die. God didn't immunize him to Satan's deceit nor protect him from Satan's presence. God actually cast fallen Lucifer down to the earth which he had created as a domicile for man. Adam's only defenses against the wiles of this usurper would be his confidence in God's person and obedience to his word.

Adam was the first stage of God's creation of man in his image. From him would come every human body ever to inhabit the earth. Later, however, in the person of Jesus Christ, the work would be finished and even the potential to sin would be done away. The New Testament tells us that Adam was made a living soul,[22] and through him would every living soul emerge. But Jesus was made a life-giving Spirit, and through him men and women would receive eternal life and be conformed to the image of God.

At the time of creation, Adam was set over the works of God's hands. Obviously he was a mature specimen of manhood. Although his responsibility was of awesome magnitude, and his authority extended to every entity of God's earthly creation, we have no record of his taking a course in political science, or horticulture. He was intuitively equipped and led by the Spirit of God. He was able to care for the trees and plants of the garden of Eden.[23] He was able to understand the characteristics of all the animals and name them appropriately.[24] He exercised absolute authority over the earthly creation of God.

He was under authority as well. God had created him for God's own purpose. It was God who commissioned him to do what he did. It was the Spirit of God that motivated this first man. There is a principle of life revealed here. Human authority is never absolute; it is derived. Adam was *in* authority as long as he was *under* the authority of God. His authority was commensurate with his submission to God's authority. We know from reading Hebrew 2:7 and Genesis 1:26-28 that Adam was given dominion over the earth. God was obviously the ruler of all creation, but the man was the visible administrator of that invisible authority.

At that point in human history the angelic creation was in place, ready to serve the man God had created for himself. The vast heavens had been filled with galaxies. The earth had been prepared to meet every need of humanity and populated with every kind of animal and plant life. Adam had been placed in authority there and was in complete and happy submission to God.

In this picture, however, the seeds of sin and rebellion existed, but only in an element of the angelic creation. Adam, so far, was still perfect and unaffected by the rebellion. There were two problems to be overcome. They were the man's potential for sin and death, and the fact that the fallen angel, Lucifer, was alive and well in the earth to which God had banished him.

Not only was Satan alive, but in his rebellion he was burning with a dedicated zeal to usurp God's authority over the man. Meanwhile, Adam had authority over everything that lived in the earth, including the serpent through whom Satan would later confront man. In that confrontation, the man was going to have the opportunity to exercise choice. We have already mentioned that the ability to choose is essential to love and obedience, the two major components of a holy relationship with God.

CHAPTER 2 References

1. Genesis 1:1
2. Isaiah 45:18
3. Genesis 1:26
4. Exodus 20:4
5. Luke 3:23-38
6. I Thesselonians 5:23
7. Romans 12:2
8. Isaiah 55:8,9
9. I Corinthians 13:12
10. Isaiah 46:10
11. Ephesians 1:11
12. Romans 8:28-34
13. Genesis 3:1-5
14. Revelation 4:11
15. Genesis 1:26; 2:7
16. Genesis 1:26
17. II Corinthians 5:17
18. I John 2:20,27
19. John 8:28,29
20. I John 3:1,2
21. Hebrews 2:7
22. I Corinthians 15:45
23. Genesis 2:15
24. Genesis 2:19

3

The Fall of Man

"God must be sentimental, perhaps even a romantic," someone said, commenting on Genesis 2:18, *"And the Lord God said, 'It is not good that the man should be alone; I will make an help meet for him'."*

There was more to God's statement, though, than mere sentiment. There was the matter of God's commission to Adam at the time of his creation, "Multiply and fill the earth."[1] We may well wonder, as perhaps Adam did, how that was to be accomplished, when God had not created two people. He had created only Adam.[2] Every person who would ever dwell on the earth was created in him and was biologically a part of him.

In the New Testament Adam is called the first man; Jesus, the second man.[3] Every one of Adam's race is referred to as "in Adam." All who have been born again are referred to as "in Christ."[4] We will discuss this relationship at length in a later chapter.

God had already determined the means of reproduction. Man was created male and female.[5] Marriage and sexual relations had been determined and sanctified before the first person was placed in the earth. Interestingly, however, God created only one being from dust. Into his nostrils God breathed the breath of life, and man became a (singular) living soul.[6]

To fulfill the commission to multiply in the earth it was necessary that Adam have a helper specifically suited to him. God brought every beast and fowl he had created before Adam to be named. But for Adam there was not found a help fit for him.[7]

God's plan was, and is, to bring many sons into glory. But how was Adam to multiply alone? There was nothing in creation outside of Adam's own body that could contribute to that process. It would have to be an act of God. So God acted:

"The Lord God caused a deep sleep to fall upon Adam, and he slept: and he took one of his ribs, and closed up the flesh instead thereof; and the rib, which the Lord God had taken from man, made he a woman, and brought her unto the man." [6]

The Sin Defined

To many in our society the story of Adam and Eve seems a myth. Song writers tell of Eve tempting Adam with an "apple" — suggesting it is a reference to sex. Many accept as fact that the first sin involved sex, implying that sex was illicit and a taboo from the beginning. Nothing could be further from the truth. God made them male and female and commanded them to multiply and fill the earth. Such a relationship, then, was obviously God's will and, according to the scriptures, the marriage bed is sanctified and undefiled.[8]

The first sin was much more fundamental and subversive to God's plan. The essence of sin is in Satan's phrase "I will be like The Most High." God, as we know, cast Lucifer down to the earth where he would one day appear in the form of a serpent in the beautiful and bountiful garden of Eden. God had filled that garden with every tree that is good for food and told Adam and Eve that they could freely eat.[9] There was provision to satisfy every need.

Beside all that, he had placed two other trees in the garden: the tree of life, and the tree of the knowledge of good and evil. Regarding the tree of life, God gave no warnings. They were welcome to eat of it. Its fruit would cause them to live forever. (The tree of life is mentioned again in the book of the Revelation in connection with the Kingdom of God. It seems to typify the Lord Jesus himself in that context.)

Regarding the tree of the knowledge of good and evil, God said, "Ye shall not eat of it. For in the day thou eatest thereof **thou shalt surely die.**" What could possibly be so deadly about eating an apple? Nothing, of course. But this was not an apple tree. This was the tree of the knowledge of good and evil.

To understand the enormity of the seemingly insignificant act of plucking the fruit of this tree and eating it, we must recall the reason for man's being. To be the body through which the invisible God would reveal *his* action and *his* character precludes any agenda or action independent of God. Adam was not to concern himself with good and evil; he was simply to respond to the will of God. The knowledge of good and evil as a basis of action would involve an entirely different relationship, especially if the acquisition of that knowledge were motivated by a desire to be an independent entity "like the Most High."

Actions determined by men based on a good versus evil value system are not the same as those determined by God and discharged by the leading of his Spirit. In the New Testament we read, "For as many as are led by the Spirit of God, they are the sons of God."[10] Adam's body was to be a vehicle to express the character of God.

There are many things that are not evil, or are even considered good, that are not the will of God. It follows, therefore, that the knowledge of good and evil is not the criterion for action, but rather "knowing what the will of the Lord is."[11] There must be a commitment to obedience in order to fulfill the will of God.

Being made in the likeness of God, Adam had within him (by God's design) a will. Now, with a direct command of God not to exercise an existing option, the man had the opportunity to choose — to obey or disobey. To obey would have been a demonstration of the will of God.[12] To disobey would be to declare independence. Such independence would result in spiritual death and an apparent frustration of God's purpose for the man. Adam, in his choice to disobey, would express a disregard for God's purpose and a willingness to frustrate God's plan in order to attain to some other agenda. That was the nature of the sin that would break his fellowship with God, place him under a different authority and bring death to his spirit.[13]

The third chapter of Genesis records the event that left Adam (and all who were in him) defeated and dead in trespasses and sin.[14] But nowhere is it recorded that this incident frustrated the plan of God. God foreknew this event and had prepared for it before the creation. (Remember that the angels were created to serve those who would be saved before there were any lost.)

The whole redemptive plan was in God's mind before the first act of creation took place. Man, who had been created in the kingdom of God without choice, by the exercise of choice would, when the opportunity came, separate himself from God. All in Adam, because of that choice—that singular act of disobedience— would be born separated from God.[15]

In Satan's rebellion against God he instigated the confrontation between Eve and the Serpent, a determination to rule over the humanity God had created for himself. God, on the other hand, was unfolding a plan that would ultimately reveal God's wisdom to all the principalities and powers: that is, the angelic beings who were looking on.[16]

A New System Called The World

The intrusion of sin into the human race came in four installments. First came the *confrontation* of the woman by the tempter; next the *communication* of Lucifer's philosophy; then the *conformity* of the man to the philosophy of sin; and, finally, the *consequences* of his sin. Let's look at this four step progression into the bondage of a new world system.

First *the confrontation*. The serpent's approach was subtle[17] yet very understandable when we consider that the word "serpent" is translated from the Hebrew word "Nachash," which means *enchanter*. Although the creature is accurately described as a serpent, it may well be as much a reference to his character as his physical appearance. He was, according to Ezekiel's description, a creature of extraordinary beauty and extreme wisdom, well able to deceive the woman, who knew nothing of sin.

34

Since he did not confront Adam directly but rather the woman, it is safe to assume that the woman, apart from her head, was more susceptible to deception. If Adam is a representation of Christ,[18] as the apostle Paul declares in the New Testament, and the woman a picture of his church, it is a fitting allegory. We, God's people, who are described as the bride of Christ, would be hard pressed to match wits with the adversary independently of our head, the Lord Jesus Christ. He is our shield and our defender.[19]

The serpent's opening remarks were designed to generate doubt about God's decree. "Hath God said ye shall not eat of every tree of the garden?" The inference is that   perhaps God is withholding something from the pair.

"We may eat of the fruit of the trees of the garden," Eve responded in defense of her Lord, "But of the fruit of the tree which is in the midst of the garden God hath said, 'ye shall not eat of it, neither shall ye touch it,' (she added), 'lest ye die.'" Eve had been subtly challenged to think thoughts that did not originate in her, and to question the validity of God's decree.[20]

The **communication** of sin's philosophy was the obvious objective of this confrontation. "You shall not surely die," the serpent answered the woman, "for God doth know that in the day ye eat thereof, then your eyes shall be opened, and ye shall be as gods, knowing good and evil."

The serpent implied that God was the liar; that somehow God would keep man from being as God; that God feared the competition that man might become. The lie was, and has always been, one can disobey God and live. It is possible to sin and not die.[21] But the fact is that the law of sin and death is built into the creation, just as is the law of gravity. Sin always brings death.

By disregarding God's prophetic warning, Satan suggested, man could be like the Most High. Far from suffering death as God had stated, the contrary would be true: man would gain the opportunity to be like God, but independent of him. Essentially Satan was introducing Adam's race to the false but popular concept that knowledge (the knowledge of good and evil) is what makes us God-like. From that day to this, man has been deceived by this philosophy of sin and of all human religions, "I can be like the Most High."

Sin and false religion are cousins. Both espouse the same philosophy: "I will be like God" by doing something or knowing something. In the case of sin, while knowing the command of God (Thou shalt not...), the sinner says, "In this case I will make my own rules. I will be like God."

In the case of religion, the participant is taught to believe that by his good works or positive thoughts, or whatever, he will become like God, or, in some cases, will *be* a god.

Then came *conformity*. Immediately, it seems, Eve was captivated, as many are today, by the magnificent thought of being like God. She stood momentarily perplexed between God's stern warning of death and Satan's enticing promise of life as a god.

Her subsequent action would be dictated by whom she believed. Until now she had believed God. There had been no thought of partaking of that tree of the knowledge of good and evil because God had said it would bring death. But now there was a question. A compelling argument had been made that God's word was not true. The truth is exactly contrary. If one partakes of the tree of the knowledge of good and evil one will live as God.

The challenge was to "repent and believe." Repent, that is, of God's truth and put faith in Satan's lie! Her new found desire became her conviction, and through repentance and faith she was converted *from* the kingdom of God *to* The kingdom of this world.

The scriptures identify the characteristics of the tree of the knowledge of good and evil. It was *good for food, beautiful to look upon*, and a tree to be *desired to make one wise*.[22] Those characteristics translate into the lust of the flesh, the lust of the eyes, and the pride of life, the three categories of sin the New Testament describes as the components of the world.[23]

The Lust of the Flesh. The woman saw that the tree was good for food. In Eve's case there was no need for food. She and Adam had every tree of the garden. There was nothing lacking to satisfy every legitimate desire and every physical appetite. This tree's fruit, however, promised to satisfy her illicit yearning for that which God had not sanctioned and was clearly not his will for them. This

The Fall of Man

defines perfectly the lust of the flesh.

The Lust of the Eyes. Despite the abundance of beauty that may surround us, nothing is as delightful to look at as that which we have set our hearts upon. That was true of Eve. Until that moment she had been satisfied with the beauty of God's garden. Perhaps she had hardly noticed the beauty of that forbidden tree because she was perfectly willing to avoid it in obedience to God's command. But now things had changed.

Suddenly, the promise of a great future attached itself to that tree, and she allowed herself to be convinced that God's words concerning it were not true. There was a source of life apart from God's tree of life. It was in this tree of knowledge of good and evil that god-likeness was to be found. Suddenly, it was, of all the trees, the most desirable. In it were the riches of visual treasure, the lust of the eye.[24]

The source of Eve's error was the lie she believed. That principle is still in force. If one believes the lies that appeal to the flesh, one is prone to disregard God's truth, to disobey God's word. The adversary injects into the heart desires that seem to promise life but, if fulfilled, bring death.

However, those who delight themselves in the Lord find the opposite to be true. As they seek him, God places desires in their hearts. The will of God, therefore, becomes the desire of their heart, and obeying him their delight.[25]

The Pride of Life. In the state of innocence that he enjoyed in fellowship with Jehovah, the Spirit of God was the center of Adam's consciousness. His actions demonstrated the will of God. God's revealed wisdom was sufficient directive for Adam, and to fulfill God's purpose was sufficient motivation. For Adam and Eve there were no goals but to obey God. No extraneous knowledge cluttered their minds, only the clear and accurate knowledge that God revealed to them. Man, who in himself was nothing apart from God, experienced God working in him to will and to cause him to do God's good pleasure.[26] Adam was perfect except for the potential of sin and death that lay buried in his human will. Should he choose to disobey God, it could separate him from God forever.

Man's environment and circumstances were ideal except for the presence of that awesome tree and the subtle personification of sin disguised in the beauty of a serpent. But now, as Eve allowed herself to be convinced by the evil one and as she looked upon the forbidden tree, she saw in it the promise of god-likeness. It would make her as wise as God. She could be like God quite independently of him.

What a challenge to be one's own Lord. What could be more exhilarating than the lordship of self: self-motivation, self-awareness, self-sufficiency, self-esteem, self-confidence? "Me", the center of the universe. "I will be like the Most High."

This self-centeredness causes man to make his own agenda the priority, to credit himself with his successes or his good fortune, and to look narrowly on his "inferiors." Self is first. This is the pride of life.

In Genesis 3:6 we read the awful words, *"She took of the fruit thereof and did eat, and gave also unto her husband with her; and he did eat."*

Sin, then, was more than eating an apple, more than an act of sex between a man and his wife. It was the tragic transition from believing and obeying God and being the vehicle through which he could demonstrate his will, to joining the rebellion of the fallen Lucifer and despising God's truth. Sin's triune nature— the lust of the flesh, the lust of the eye, and the pride of life—had been imparted to man. He had been confronted by the adversary, motivated by the philosophy of sin, and had acted upon it. The potential of sin had been fulfilled.

The *consequence* of Adam's sin has affected every man in every generation. It has plagued, conquered and destroyed every person born of Adam's race, great and small. All have succumbed to its ultimate wage, death. The death sentence rests upon every member of Adam's race.[27] People live either in terror of God's judgment or in willing ignorance of it. Regardless of how they cope, by denial or resignation, God has declared, "There is none righteous, no not one."[28] "For all have sinned and come short of the glory of God,"[29] and, "the wages of sin is death."[30]

For 930 years Adam lived and produced children.[31] All of them bore the image of their father, who no longer bore the image of God. He was now a fallen, natural man, spiritually dead in trespasses and sin and unable to fellowship with God. That was the image they bore. That sin nature dictated the bent of their actions. Humanity's willing participation in sin has, for all the generations of history, borne witness to the universally sinful nature of fallen man.

CHAPTER 3 References

1. Genesis 1:28
2. Genesis 2:7
3. I Corinthians 15:47
4. I Corinthians 15:22; II Corinthians 5:17
5. Genesis 1:27
6. Genesis 2:21,22
7. Genesis 2:7
8. Genesis 2:20
9. Hebrews 13:4
10. Genesis 2:8-17
11. Romans 8:14
12. Ephesians 5:17
13. Romans 12:2
14. Genesis 2:17
15. Ephesians 2:1,2
16. Romans 5:19
17. Ephesians 3:10
18. Genesis 3:1
19. Romans 5:14
20. Ps.33:20
21. Genesis 3:1-3
22. Genesis 3:4,5
23. Genesis 3:6
24. I John 2:15-17
25. Matthew 6:19
26. Psalm 37:4
27. Philippians 2:13
28. Romans 5:12
29. Romans 3:10
30. Romans 3:23
31. Romans 6:23
32. Genesis 5:3-5

Chapter 4

The Consequences of Sin
and the Resulting World System

There is more to death than meets the eye. Whatever Adam had thought "You shall surely die" meant, his unbelief had left him unprepared for the consequences of his sin. Their eyes were indeed opened, just as the serpent had promised, but they were devastated by what they saw.

Until that moment, Eve had seen in Adam, not a naked man, but the image of the invisible God, crowned with glory and honor and set majestically over all the works of God's hands. He was clothed with God-likeness. Because she was bone of his bone and flesh of his flesh,[1] Adam saw in Eve that same image. That's the way it had been from the time God had wakened him from his deep sleep to present to him his bride.

Nothing in his imagination made him think that image would change except, perhaps, for the better when their eyes would be opened and they would be as gods. Then suddenly their eyes were opened.[2] Everything was different. They realized their nakedness and were aghast at the comparative repulsiveness of naked flesh. The glory of God was gone. The vibrancy of godly life had given way to the repugnance of spiritual death.

41

Suddenly they were *self* conscious. They had always been physically naked, but they had never been ashamed.[3] Now their nakedness embarrassed them. They were not as gods. They seemed to be more like the animals than like God. All sense of satisfaction was gone. They could not accept themselves this way. But there was the terrifying realization that there was no way back—ever. Self-consciousness immediately produced a need for self-improvement. They must, therefore, do something to cover themselves.[4]

Neither Adam, nor any in Adam, would ever again be as he had been: mindless of self, in fellowship and satisfied with God. God had never accused him of shortcoming or mentioned his nakedness. On the contrary, Adam was crowned with glory and honor and set over the works of God's hands.[5]

That was all gone now. Instead, he had become Satan's dupe, stripped of glory, embarrassed by his nakedness, conscious of his own uncomeliness, and scrambling to cover himself from the eyes of God. Adam was now conscious only of his flesh. Before his disobedience he had lived in the spirit, an entirely different realm. But now he was spiritually dead. As God had warned him, the day he ate of the tree of the knowledge of good and evil he died.

Since then, how many of us have stumbled because of self-consciousness, been defeated by embarrassment, or beaten by our shame of what we are? That's not because we are less than others; it's simply part of Adam's legacy. It is a result of sin.

The world's populace still suffers from these symptoms of spiritual death; unhappy with what they are, many people seek in vain for a remedy that does not exist. Suffering from the guilt their sinful nature has produced, they turn to psychology or humanistic religion for relief. Some find none. Others are convinced that their behavior is normal (everyone is like that to some degree). Still others discover their problem is rooted in someone else's failures. Some are taught there is no such thing as sin. Nothing is right or wrong. Everyone has to do whatever it takes to find oneself, therefore one should feel no guilt.

Because they live in the serpent's deception (I will be like the Most High), out of touch with the Spirit of God, they seek human remedies to escape the misery of their fallen nature. With a band-aid of false but comforting counsel some manage happily in their spiritual death.

* * * * *

The moment I wrote *spiritual death*, I remembered the challenge by a young man in a meeting a few years ago. "What do you mean by spiritual death?" he asked. "Death is death. Adam died within a thousand years of the time he ate the apple. That's what God meant. He said a thousand years is a day. If he meant a twenty four hour day, obviously he was wrong. It didn't happen."

Let's talk about spiritual death. The following diagram represents man as God created him: spirit, soul and body, a human trinity. God is a Spirit, and it was with the living spirit of man that God communed. Man's spirit, under the direction of God, controlled the man's soul (mind, will, and emotions). His soul, in turn, dictated the actions of his body. In this condition the activity of Adam's body perfectly reflected the input of the Spirit of God.

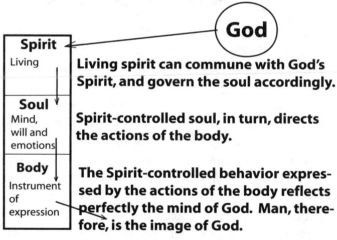

Spirit — Living	Living spirit can commune with God's Spirit, and govern the soul accordingly.
Soul — Mind, will and emotions	Spirit-controlled soul, in turn, directs the actions of the body.
Body — Instrument of expression	The Spirit-controlled behavior expressed by the actions of the body reflects perfectly the mind of God. Man, therefore, is the image of God.

But sin entered the scene. The man, repenting from God, placed his trust in the lie of Satan. The result of that broken fellowship was death to man's spirit as demonstrated in the next diagram. From that point on, the input to man's soul came from the world through his senses. Now his actions would reflect perfectly the world's good and evil value system, acquired through eating of the tree of the knowledge of good and evil, rather than the will of God. The apostle Paul referred to this condition when he said "Ye were dead in trespasses and sin".

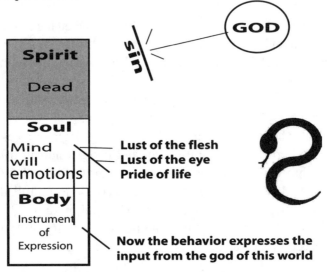

This is the reason Jesus said, "Except a man be *born again*" of the Spirit, he cannot see [discern] or enter into, the kingdom of God.[6] This rebirth, obviously, is not physical. It takes place in a person's spirit.

* * * * *

"Hide! God must not see us like this," must have been Adam's alarming cry. Genesis 3:8 says, *"They heard the voice of the Lord God walking in the garden in the cool of the day, and Adam and his wife hid themselves from the presence of the Lord amongst the trees of the garden."*

When God called them, Adam confessed, *"I heard thy voice in the garden and I was afraid because I was naked; and I hid myself."*[7]

Adam, no longer a spiritual man, could not stand in the presence of a holy God. He was soulish. For Adam and Eve, the voice of God no longer meant communion but conviction. God's presence no longer meant fellowship but fear. Fallen man was now eager to avoid the Holy Spirit, to separate himself from God's words.

The seed of this spiritually dead man, Adam, populates the

earth today, bearing his image[8] and perpetuating Adam's attitude toward God. That's why people are often dissatisfied with themselves today. Some spend a hundred dollars an hour (more or less) for psychotherapy, when the root problem is not the psyche [soul] but the spirit.

They would change themselves if they could, but they can't. Therefore they spend their time and their money in an effort to be at peace with their nature. But because that nature is contrary to God they must either try to avoid him or redefine him, to make a god compatible with their fallen nature.[9]

For Adam, the trees of the garden were God's blessing. Every material need was provided through them.[10] But now that Adam's fellowship with God was broken by sin,[11] he hid himself behind those very blessings. Things haven't changed. The Bible says God gives power to get wealth.[12] That is one of God's blessings. But for the *natural* man, the more he gains (or sets his mind on gaining), the more materialistic he becomes and the less he seeks after God. God's material blessings become a barrier to hide behind.[13]

The Woman's Curse

As a result of the severed relationship with God, there were additional consequences of sin. Women were now to bring forth children in sorrow.[14] It would appear, from observing human history, that this curse included more than merely the travail of childbirth. That was only the beginning.

Through sin a horrendous system had been set in motion. Women would bear children who would fall to the swords of enemy armies. Men would become cannon fodder, and their families would succumb to famine and disease. Children would be snatched from their mothers arms and sold into slavery; others would experience every kind of inhumanity. Behind every sufferer there is an agonizing mother. It will continue to be so as long as sin has dominion over the human race.

In addition to these sorrows, God told the woman that her desire would be toward her husband and that he would *rule* over her. No such relationship existed before the fall. The woman was one with her husband, literally bone of his bone and flesh of his flesh. The

45

harmony resulting from their single-minded performance of God's will precluded any need for domination or authoritarianism.

Sin changed all that. The man would now *rule* over the woman. This wicked condition of fallen humanity has given way to escalating abuse on the one hand and increasing rebellion on the other. Where Christ is not honored and God's Word not obeyed, men's abuse of women often causes smoldering resentment or open rebellion. This vicious circle is a desecration of the picture of the love between Jesus Christ and his church that marriage is meant to be.[15]

Throughout the world today, where women have not been liberated by the emancipating Gospel of Christ, abuse by cruel and dominating men is an accepted norm.

Even in so-called Christian nations, where the Word of God is not honored and Christ is not recognized as Lord, rebellion against male "rule" has produced a "liberation" that is characterized by an unhealthy independence; in many cases even role reversal. It has destroyed the security of marriage, the responsibility of family, and even the sanctity of life. It is a grotesque caricature of the liberation that the righteousness of Christ brings and has produced an almost incredible measure of anguish.

The Man's Curse

The man also was cursed as a result of sin. To him God said in Genesis 3:17-19, *"Because thou hast hearkened unto the voice of thy wife, and hast eaten of the tree, of which I commanded thee saying, thou shalt not eat of it: cursed is the ground for thy sake; in sorrow shalt thou eat of it all the days of thy life; thorns also, and thistles shall it bring forth to thee; and thou shalt eat the herb of the field; in the sweat of thy face shalt thou eat bread, till thou return unto the ground; for out of it wast thou taken: for dust thou art and unto dust shalt thou return."*

The ground that had yielded only God's blessing would bring forth a new crop. Thistles would intrude into man's agriculture, increasing his labors and diminishing his harvests. Thorns would compete for the land.

One day someone would fashion a crown of these thorns and

press it upon the head of the Righteous One who was to come to deliver man from the curse of sin. How ironic: the Righteous One would be crowned with the curse for which the unrighteous one was responsible.

Thorns, thistles, sweat, sorrow: these are the key words defining the lot of fallen man. Whereas God had once said that of every tree they might *freely* eat, now man would sweat to eat and toil to survive. The demands of his flesh would occupy all his time. His needs would drive him, his *things* would own him and his appetites consume him. His life would perish and he would end as dust.[16]

What a dreary hope. Jesus made reference to this when he said, "After all these *things* do the gentiles seek."[17] [emphasis added].

Man, who had been created to manifest the image of God, was now a marred, broken vessel, unsuited for that purpose. He must be barred from the tree of life lest, in that fallen condition, he should eat and live forever. Genesis 3:23,24 notes, "... *therefore the Lord God sent him forth from the garden of Eden to till the ground from whence he was taken. So he drove out the man; and he placed at the east of the garden of Eden Cherubim, and a flaming sword which turned every way to keep the way of the tree of life.*"

Before any man could partake of that tree of life, God's righteous judgments would have to be satisfied. It was not compatible with God's purpose that fallen man, living after the flesh and dead in his spirit, should have eternal life in the Kingdom of God.

Though originally consisting of a living spirit, soul, and body, man had, when his spirit died, become something less than the humanity God had created. By God's standard he had become sub-human. Perhaps this explains the thinking and behavior of so many members of the "human" race.

Adam's disobedience initiated a whole new system of things. It is called "the world." To some, "world" may seem to be simply another term for "the earth." However, "earth" is a reference to the planet upon which we live – part of the physical creation; while "the world" is usually a reference to the system imposed upon earth's inhabitants. The Bible teaches us that "the earth is the Lord's, and the fullness thereof."[18] But the same Bible teaches us that Satan is

47

the god of this world.[19]

Before Adam ate the fruit of the knowledge of good and evil, God was his only authority. No will but God's was exercised. By God's decree all things were under Adam's hand, and what Adam did expressed God's will. The whole earthly creation under God was governed by the man. What could more clearly depict the kingdom of God?

In this happy state, man enjoyed briefly the abundant and automatic provision of God. He knew nothing of death, pain or sorrow. None of those would come until sin came. Even as a potential sinner, Adam began his existence by experiencing what the saved ones will realize when God's plan is finished and the potential to sin no longer exists.[20]

The world system, with it's suffering and death, resulted from Adam's defection. By his disobedience he surrendered his dominion to the serpent. Adam was persuaded to disobey God and thus joined Satan's rebellion. By repenting *from* God's truth and placing his faith in Satan's lie, Adam worshipped a created being rather than the creator. Satan became man's god, seized Adam's God-given authority over the earthly creation, and became the god of this world.

A New Order

Under this new regime, Adam was a new creature. He and his offspring expressed a new mentality. Man became egocentric, a lover of self, covetous, proud, unthankful, without self-control, fierce, treacherous.[21] He was (and is) guided by the lust of the flesh, the lust of the eye, and the pride of life.[22] Things, rather than the will of God, became the object of his pursuit. Materialism became his guiding principle.

The apostle Paul would later describe this fallen humanity as "natural man" because such a man is spiritually dead, unable to see or know God. He no longer hears God's voice nor, in some cases, even believes that God exists. If he does assent to God's existence, he sees no need to acknowledge him as his Lord. He believes his own will is equal to that of God's. And no wonder, because, as natural man, he "cannot receive the things of the spirit of God; for they are foolishness unto him; neither can he know them because they are spiritually discerned."[23]

In his rebellious act of disobedience against God's Lordship, Adam unwittingly pledged himself inextricably to the evil authority of Satan, the god of this world. Man was lost by an act of his will. But in spite of the misery his rebellion incurred, he could not will himself saved again.[24] His fall was irreversible.

The magnitude of the tragedy is staggering. Every person who was created in Adam fell in Adam. Since then, every one of his descendants has been born, without choice, in the image of his fallen father—natural man, separated from God. Nothing any man can do will alter that fact or change that relationship.

This is so important that it is a key fact to comprehending the gospel. To most of us the word "grace" means unmerited favor. It means that I have been given something that I could not have achieved or acquired by any merit of my own. We understand from the New Testament that that's how individuals are delivered from this quagmire of sin in which they find themselves because of Adam's fall.

It was by a kind of grace in reverse that we descendants of Adam were made sinners in the first place. We received that nature, without any "merit" of our own. We did no act to qualify as sinners. We were born that way. We were born in the image of our fallen father, Adam. Through a singular act of disobedience by our father Adam, we were made sinners.

The central theme of the Bible is encapsulated in this text in Romans 5:19.

"For as by one man's disobedience (Adam's sin) *many were made sinners, so by the obedience of one* (Jesus) *shall many be made righteous."*

We were lost by the "grace" of one man. It is entirely logical, therefore, that we must look to the grace of another to save us from that condition. We cannot undo what we did not do in the first place.

From Adam's fall to the present, humanity lies wrecked in the icy grip of sin and death. Where, then, is God's purpose now? It is still intact. God's plan is not ruined nor is God frustrated. It was necessary that man exercise the will God gave him. However, the result of Adam's choice was death and that choice has placed natural man out of God's fellowship; but certainly not out of his reach. There is a positive side to this tragedy. Because of it, attributes of God which could have been made manifest under no other circumstances have been revealed to us. God has expressed those marvelous attributes of his character: boundless grace, incomprehensible compassion, forgiveness and enduring mercy – all in response to our dire need. The revelation of these attributes of God required human failure. Through that failure man became the object of God's grace. That will lift him to heights of perfectness in Christ that could never have been known in Adam.

Originally Adam was in fellowship with God by no choice of his own. When given the power to choose, he opted to disobey and escape God's presence. As a result, all, including you and me, were born outside of God's fellowship. We were *made* sinners.

Through his redemptive plan, which was in place before the first word of creation was ever uttered, God opened the way back. All who would respond willingly and joyfully to the grace he proffered would ultimately be conformed to his image and enjoy his presence forever. These, then, who respond to his grace, appreciate his mercy, and experience his forgiveness, will be the humanity in the image of God of which he spoke in Genesis 1:26. These will constitute the body through whom God will manifest himself forever.

CHAPTER 4 References

1. Genesis 2:23
2. Genesis 3:7
3. Genesis 2:25
4. Genesis 3:7
5. Hebrews 2:7
6. John 3:3,5
7. Genesis 3:10
8. Genesis 5:3
9. Romans 1:21-28
10. Genesis 2:9
11. Isaiah 59:2
12. Deuteronomy 8:17,18
13. I Timothy 6:9,10
14. Genesis 3:16
15. Ephesians 5:22-31
16. Genesis 3:19
17. Matthew 6:31,32
18. I Corinthians 10:26
19. II Corinthians 4:4
20. Revelation 21:4
21. I Timothy 3:2,3
22. I John 2:16
23. I Corinthians 2:14
24. John 6:44

God's Eternal Purpose

5
The Last Adam

The first Adam failed. So enormous are the consequences of that failure that they are incomprehensible to the people who reap its results. Adam had been created in the image of God. But he acquiesced to the serpent and introduced sin into the world. By sin came death, which passed upon all of Adam's descendants.[1] According to the testimony of scripture, in all of Adam's race, "there is none righteous, no not one."[2] "There is not a just man upon the earth that doeth good and sinneth not."[3]

To look for a savior among those of Adam's fallen race would be a vain search. There was none among them who could save himself, much less someone else. So, even as the curse on sin was being pronounced, God promised a savior. As he cursed Satan he said, *"I will put enmity between thee and the woman, and between thy seed and her seed; it shall bruise thy head, and thou shalt bruise his heel."*[4]

Perhaps the meaning of this declaration was not immediately clear to Adam or to his wife. They lived for 930 years without seeing anything that resembled the fulfillment of God's statement. But in retrospect, we can see the remarkable fulfillment of this first promise of a redeemer.

From the very beginning, God made it clear that it would be another man who would reverse the tragic consequence of the first man's sin. God's Word declares in the New Testament that by man came death, and by man came the resurrection from the dead.[5]

The savior was to be the seed of the woman, a human being born of a human mother. And he would bruise the serpent's head. In the course of history, the meaning of the bruised heel became clear. The serpent, Satan, would be defeated and destroyed. But in destroying him, the seed of the woman would also suffer.

The fulfillment of that promise would be in God's due time. Meanwhile, on the canvas of history, God painted innumerable pictures describing his redemptive plan, so that when the savior would come his identity and his program would be unmistakable to all whose hearts were prepared to receive him.

Soon after their expulsion from the garden of Eden, a son was born to Adam and Eve. Adam had been created in the image of God, alive in spirit and able to be God's perfect vessel. However, Cain was born in Adam's fallen image, dead in trespasses and sin. From birth, therefore, he was something less than the humanity that God had originally made.

Another son followed. Eve named him Abel.[6] He was a shepherd, and apparently tender hearted toward God. He is described in the New Testament as a righteous man. In many respects he foreshadowed Jesus, the good shepherd. The brief story of these two brothers sets the stage for the unfolding history that comprises the Bible message.

Although Cain is described as evil, he was apparently religious, because he voluntarily brought a sacrifice to God. By occupation he was a farmer. Abel also brought a sacrifice. His was the firstling of his flocks—a sacrifice of blood. God had respect for Abel's sacrifice, but not for Cain's. As a result Cain became angry with God.

"Why are you wroth, and why is your countenance fallen?" God asked. "If you do well, shall you not be accepted?"[6]

God's language indicates that the door was still open for Cain. God did not say, "You would have been accepted if you had done well." He was ready to receive Cain if he were willing to ask God what was acceptable and then would do it.

Cain could have acquired from Abel, the good shepherd, a sacrifice that would have pleased God. But he would not yield to any way but his own. He expected God to be satisfied with whatever seemed good in Cain's eyes. He was willing to serve God only in a way that pleased himself, not in a way that required submission to God's will or a humbling of himself before another man.

Cain's hatred was kindled toward the man that God approved, so when he met Abel in the field, he slew him. The analogy is clear. The religious man killed the righteous shepherd who had made the acceptable sacrifice to God. That scenario is played out through all of prophetic history. Israel slew the prophets that God sent. When Jesus, the good shepherd, finally came, the religious leaders raged against him in jealousy and demanded his death. From the very beginning, God made it clear how his redemptive program would unfold. The savior and the plan were to be unmistakably identifiable.

Time marched on from the days of Cain and Abel. Sin increased for several generations, until the whole earth was filled with violence and all flesh had corrupted itself.[7] God determined to destroy every person from the face of the earth. In doing so, however, he must keep his promise of a savior. Another picture would result. God's wrath and God's mercy would be revealed. His judgment and his grace would be demonstrated in a remarkable way that would once again foreshadow salvation.

Although all flesh had corrupted itself, one man found grace in the eyes of the Lord.[8] Through grace, Noah was made righteous and upright in his generation. God told him to build an ark, a great ship covered within and without with pitch which would waterproof it and shield those within from the raging waters outside. Noah obeyed by faith, and while he demonstrated his faith by his works, he also preached righteousness[9] in the midst of a corrupted and hostile generation. No one in the whole earth apart from his own family believed him.

The sin of Noah's generation and their rejection of the Word of God which he preached, precipitated the wrath of God. As a result,

God sent a flood which destroyed the wicked. Only those eight souls who entered the ark were saved from the judgment of God.

The ark is a picture of Christ. The pitch that waterproofed the ark represents the blood of Christ, the covering, which makes those who are in Christ judgment-proof. That ark was the window through which the lineage of Christ, the seed of the woman, was preserved. Not only the line of the redeemer but also that of all the redeemed was saved through the obedience of one man, by the grace of God. In that historic event we have a preview of the coming judgment of the world, and the salvation of those in Christ who have believed God's Word.

Approximately 450 years passed, and people again multiplied upon the earth. Then God chose a man named Abraham. He promised him that through his seed would "all the nations of the earth be blessed."[10] The seed of the woman, then, was also to be the seed of Abraham. Again God spoke to Abraham saying, "In Isaac shall thy seed be called."[11] The prophetic focus was narrowed, therefore, to the lineage of Isaac.

When Isaac's wife, Rebekah, was with child, God revealed to them that twins were in her womb. "The elder shall serve the younger,"[12] he declared. "Jacob have I loved [chosen], and Esau have I hated [rejected]."

Step by step, generation after generation, God unfolded the genealogy of the man who was to be the savior of the world. He would come with credentials. He would be the fulfillment of precise prophecies which would unfold century after century.

Before his death, Jacob prophesied that the promised savior would come through his son Judah. Then, as the nation of Israel was established and its history progressed, God revealed that the Messiah would be a descendant of King David.[13] Later, Isaiah prophesied that he would be born of a virgin.[14] Then the prophet Micah told us where: in Bethlehem of Judea.[15]

Not only was his lineage accurately reported in advance, but all the details of ceremonial law pointed in minutely detailed types and shadows to God's method of redemption. The sacrifices, the priestly responsibilities, even the religious feasts, embodied a detailed explanation of God's redemptive program.

The law, as delivered to Moses, played a part in making known the need for salvation. It defined the righteousness of God, and imparted the knowledge of sin. It imposed guilt upon the transgressors.[16] The law could not make anyone righteous, but it revealed man's sin and his need of a savior.

The law required blood sacrifices from those who sinned. Because the wages of sin is always death, the people were to understand that sin was to be dealt with either by the death of the sinner or the death of a substitute. Without the shedding of blood there is no remission of sin.[17]

All the sacrificial types and shadows were designed to make the sinner understand that a God of justice cannot excuse sin. He can forgive it when it has been atoned for, but he cannot excuse it. It is obvious that the blood of bulls and goats cannot take away sin. Those sacrifices were simply a picture. Someone was coming to make the acceptable sacrifice once for all.

That time finally came. Jesus was born to a virgin, a descendant of King David, in the town of Bethlehem in the province of Judea. A descendant of Jacob, of the seed of Abraham, he was the promised seed of the woman who was to crush the serpent's head. In the process, however, exactly as the scriptures had said, he himself would be wounded to death, and his blood would make atonement for the sins of many.

In Colossians 2:17 the apostle Paul wrote. "[The feast days and all the incumbent ceremonies and sacrifices] *are a shadow of things to come; but the body is of Christ.*" To get the picture of what that means, imagine yourself standing on the east side of a tall building about the time the sun is setting in the west. The shadows are lengthening. You hear the footsteps of someone walking east on the north side of the building. You can't see him, but as you look to the north you can see his shadow paralleling that of the building and growing longer with the sound of each step. Several things about this shadow are familiar, and you wait with anticipation to see who is casting it. Suddenly, as you watch, the object of that shadow emerges around the corner of the building. When he comes in full view you recognize him.

That's the point of the apostle Paul's statement. The components of the law of the Old Testament were the shadow that was visible for centuries before the body came into view. But when the body did appear, it was Christ. He was the one of whom all the prophets spoke. He was the blood sacrifice. He was the seed of the woman. When he came into public view, the prophet John the Baptist pointed to him and cried, "Behold the lamb of God that takes away the sin of the world."[18]

Now we must look to Jesus, God's only begotten Son. He came into the world specifically to die for every person who was condemned in Adam. The apostle Paul described Jesus as the *last Adam*. Last means the "final one." As Adam was the first man in the human race, Jesus, in God's view, was the last: the final Adam.[19]

As all people were created in the first Adam, they would be terminated in the last Adam. As far as God was concerned, when Jesus would die, all of Adam's seed would be put to death. God's dealings with Adam's corrupt race would be over.[20] They would be separated from God forever, and God's quarrel with man would end.

To accomplish this plan, Jesus must be a sacrifice without blemish. If he should be guilty of sin the result would be different. He would die, as all of Adam's race have died, for his own sin alone. Jesus was to pass under the flaming sword of God's judgment and open the way to the tree of life. To die for all and be raised again, he must live without blemish.

The scriptures state repeatedly that Jesus is the savior. In the Old Testament God said, *"I am he, before me there was no God formed, neither shall there be after me. I am the LORD [Jehovah]; and beside me there is no savior."*[21]

This man, then, is not only a human being but the incarnation of God, the creator. God, who exists eternally, created all things by his word; and Jesus Christ, the last Adam, is described by the apostle John as the Word of God made flesh. He wrote, *"In the beginning was the Word, and The Word was with God, and the Word was God. The same was in the beginning with God. All things were made by him; and without him was not anything made that was made. In him was life, and the life was the light of men.*[22] *". . .And the Word was made flesh and dwelt among us, and we beheld his glory, the glory as of the only begotten of the Father, full of grace and truth."*[23]

Many religious teachers and self-proclaimed gurus have cluttered the stage of history. Jesus was not one of them. He was the incarnate Word of God. He alone was able to accomplish the two goals for which he came into the world.

The first was to manifest the Father, the very purpose for which God had created humanity in the first place. When Jesus prayed to the Father shortly before his death, he said: *"I have glorified thee on the earth; I have finished the work which thou gavest me to do. . .I have manifested thy name to the men which thou gavest me out of the world."*[24]

Those men who lived and traveled with Jesus saw in his character, and in all the works that he did, the express image of the Father. As the scripture says: *"No man hath seen God at any time; [but] the only begotten Son,. . .he has declared [fully revealed] him."*[25]

The second objective was to save sinners. Jesus said of himself, "The Son of Man is come to seek and to save that which was lost."[26] All of humanity had been lost in Adam's fall. Now, instead of being in the image of God, people were born into the world dead in trespasses and sin. Access to the Tree of Life had been lost by Adam. Jesus had come to restore that access. The birth of Jesus Christ was as significant as was the creation of Adam. Jesus Christ is pivotal in history because he alone reversed the tragedy of Adam's fall.

We have seen that God promised a savior whom he called "the seed of the woman." The prophets who described his ancestry and the place and details of his birth made it clear that the Lord Jesus was to be a descendent of Adam; a real human being who would bear the likeness of sinful flesh. He had to be the same kind of man Adam had been before the fall. The Bible says, *"Since by man came death, by man came also the resurrection from the dead."*[27]

There are folks who fail to see the significance of fundamental truth concerning Jesus Christ. One clergyman told me that the idea of a virgin birth is unscientific and ludicrous. It didn't matter, he said, if Jesus came as an apple on a tree as long as he came. After all, he came to be a teacher and an example, so who cares how he got here.

Nothing could be further from the truth. Without a man to be our savior who himself was not a sinner by birth, all hope of eternal physical life in the presence of God would be gone. For this reason, it was imperative that Jesus be born by a human mother. It was also imperative that he be born without the inherited nature of a human father.

I will not attempt a medical treatise on what attributes derive from which parent. Others have ably undertaken that project.[28] The purpose here is to simply state what is made apparent through scripture. The seed of the woman gives substance to the physical body. Without that seed, no matter what contribution a father might make, there can be no human body. The fallen human nature that would affect the character of that human body once it came to life, however, derives from the father.[29]

Jesus was to be, in every respect, human. He was, in fact, as we have noted, a physical descendant of Adam through Abraham, Isaac, Jacob, David, Mary, and all the intervening generations. The New Testament describes him as the seed of Abraham and as the seed of David. He called himself the Son of Man. I reiterate this to emphasize the fact that Jesus was, in every respect, a human being with every potential that Adam had when he was placed upon the earth as the image of God.

There was, however, one difference between Adam before the fall and Jesus in his humanity. Whereas Adam was *created* by God, Jesus is the only *begotten* Son of God.[30] Jesus was not a created being. He was born of man after the flesh but he was begotten of God his Father. Therefore, although he emphasized his humanity by referring to himself as the Son of Man, he is described, as well, throughout the New Testament as the Son of God.

The word *begotten* is very important when referring to Jesus' sonship. It is not biblically sound to say that God gave (or sacrificed) his only son. There are many who are described in the Bible as sons of God. Adam is referred to in the gospel of Luke as the Son of God.[31] The book of Job in the Old Testament refers to sons of God.[32] All who have put their trust in Jesus and have experienced the miracle of rebirth are called sons of God.[33] But Jesus Christ is the *only* **begotten** Son of God. The particulars concerning his virgin birth are clearly spelled out in the prophets and in the Gospels.[34]

In His Appointed Time God Revealed His Redemptive Plan:

God sent the angel Gabriel, to a virgin named Mary, in the city of Nazareth. She was engaged to a man named Joseph. They were both of the house of David. The angel said to Mary, *"Hail, thou that are highly favored, the Lord is with thee."* Mary was troubled. And the angel said to her, *"Fear not, Mary, for you shall bring forth a son and shall call his name Jesus. He shall be great and shall be called the Son of the Highest . . . The Holy Ghost shall come upon thee, and the power of the Highest shall overshadow thee: Therefore that holy thing that shall be born of thee shall be called The Son of God."* [Paraphrased from Luke 2]

Jesus' body, obviously, had a beginning and, in the course of his life, would die. As a human being, his life began at his conception in Mary's womb. Before the birth of that human body, however, he was the Word of God in the bosom of the Father;[35] eternal, invisible, immortal. But now, by taking on himself mortal flesh, he laid aside his prerogative to act as God and took upon himself, instead, the form of a servant (one whose work is to *obey*), and was made in the likeness of man:[36] *the Son of Man.* Through human birth he had become the man God meant man to be.

As the eternal Word of God he was the essence and expression of the Father—of his will, his power, his righteousness. But now, made flesh, he would still express those attributes, but as a human being. If one would desire to see God, one could simply look at Jesus. He is the express image of the invisible God.[37] He is what God meant man to be.

For this reason, Jesus is sometimes referred to as "The God-man." Although many would feel that is an accurate description, it tends to be misleading. It suggests that he was not exactly human as all of Adam's race are human. Perhaps he is a super-man; half God, half man; someone with whom we can hardly identify. Perhaps in his own independent power he can walk on water, raise the dead and do other things that human beings can't.

But according to his own words Jesus did not come as a super-man. He came as a helpless man. Twice in the fifth chapter of John he said, *"Of myself I can do nothing."*[38] We can identify with that. And that is precisely why Jesus came: to identify with us where we are. Although the scriptures make it clear that Jesus was indeed God manifest in the flesh, the term "God-man" never appears in them.

Jesus was not fifty percent God and fifty percent man. We must comprehend the incomprehensible, that Jesus was one hundred percent God and one hundred percent man. To do so, we must examine the aspects of his deity and his humanity separately. God is not flesh and flesh is not God. Yet, in this entirely human being, God dwelt and walked and manifested himself[39] in the way that God intended when he created humanity.

Jesus' human nature is not a fallen nature like ours. His is like that which God created in Adam *before* the fall. The fact that Adam is called the first Adam[40] and Jesus is described as the last Adam indicates the likeness of their humanity. Adam was tempted to act independently of God and to exercise his own will. He succumbed and died. Jesus was to be tempted in the same way. Obviously, then, he must have the same potential. But Adam fell; Jesus didn't. Adam's act was called *disobedience*. Jesus' was called *obedience*.[41]

As we have noted earlier, obedience requires the option of disobedience. Acts of sin are an exercise of the will, just as obedience and disobedience are acts of the will. Jesus, possessed a human will, even as he possessed a human nature. The Father, who knows the end from before the beginning, knew that Jesus, the unblemished lamb of God, would not sin. But the Bible makes it clear that he came "in the likeness of sinful flesh."[42] Jesus came into the world with the same potential as Adam. He had PSD (the potential of sin and death). Without that potential, he could not have died, nor could he have taken upon himself our sins.

Clearly, he came with a human will – the capacity to choose, to obey or disobey. On several occasions Jesus himself made reference to this. *"I came down from heaven," he said, "not to do my own will, but the will of him that sent me."*[43]

Two wills are involved here; *my own* (human) *will* and *the will* (divine) *of him that sent me.* It is evident that, although Jesus always did the will of his Father, the potential to do otherwise was there. Jesus expressed his purpose of heart in two distinct determinations: The first, to *not* do *his own will*; secondly, to do the *will of him that sent him.* Clearly, to do the father's will while rejecting the temptation to do his own, was a choice that Jesus made.

Since Jesus was our example as well as our savior, there is something for us to learn here. The reason for our sometimes vain struggle to accomplish what we believe to be the Father's will is our failure to first purpose in our hearts not to do our own will.

Jesus never attempted to do his Father's will as an appendage to his own. Nor should we. His will was completely subjugated to that of his Father. No wonder, then, that Jesus, agonizing in the garden of Gethsemane over the terror of his impending crucifixion, cried out to the Father, *"If it be thy will let this cup pass from me. Nevertheless, not my will, but thine be done."*[44] Jesus, the man, deliberately *chose* to do the Father's will rather than his own. That's what taking up the cross is all about.

Our salvation lies, not in the fact that Jesus was a deified figure who *could* not sin. Precisely the opposite. He was a human figure who *did* not sin. It was by an act of obedience on the part of a man that we are saved, as opposed to an act of disobedience on the part of another man that we were lost. In both cases the choice of the man is in view.

From his birth Jesus was aware of his role. When he came into the world he said, *"I come to do thy will, O God."*[45] At the age of twelve Jesus went to Jerusalem with Joseph and Mary to attend a feast. When they had fulfilled the days, as they returned, the child Jesus tarried behind in Jerusalem. Joseph and Mary mistakenly supposing him to have been in the company, went a day's journey before they missed him. They returned to Jerusalem, and after seeking him three days they found him in the temple, sitting among the doctors, both hearing them and asking them questions. And all that heard him were astonished at his understanding and answers. Mary and Joseph were amazed; and Jesus' mother said, *"Son, why hast thou thus dealt with us? Behold, thy father and I have sought thee, sorrowing."*

And he said unto them, *"How is it that ye sought me? Knew ye not that I should be about my Father's business?"*[46]

Even as a boy, Jesus was uniquely preoccupied with the will of his Father. He was his Father's only begotten son. All other men, even as children, expressed in their bodies the nature and the will of their fallen father, Adam. Jesus, however, being born of God, expressed the will of his Father.

For the next eighteen years Jesus lived among his siblings – four brothers and at least two sisters—all born to Mary after Jesus was born. He was known as "the carpenter's son,"[47] and "the carpenter."[48] He experienced, therefore, every phase of life that every other man would experience: the authority of parents, the give and take of brothers and sisters, apprenticeship, life as a tradesman and, in all probability, the rigors of a small business. It was all necessary because he had to be tempted in everything as we are tempted, yet he would emerge without sin.[49]

Facing Temptation

Being in his humanity what Adam had been before the fall, inevitably he had to meet the same tempter and the same temptations that had precipitated the fall of Adam. Adam had faced the lust of the flesh, the lust of the eyes, and the pride of life as served up by the serpent himself. He had failed. Jesus, too, must face the same trial—but succeed.

At about thirty years of age he was baptized by John the Baptist in the Jordan River. When he came up out of the water the Holy Spirit descended upon him like a dove, anointing him for the peculiar ministry for which the Father had sent him.

Immediately after his anointing, the Spirit led him into the wilderness specifically to be tempted by the Devil.[50] For forty days, without food to eat, he waited, alone, in the parched wilderness. At the end of those days his weakened body cried out for food. In this emaciated condition he faced the tempter – not as God, but as man. God cannot be tempted with evil.[51]

The Devil said, "If you are the Son of God, command these stones to be made bread."[52]

Surely, as the Son of God, it was in his power to turn stones into bread to satisfy his starving flesh. But no, Jesus was not there to prove that he was the Son of God; nor to satisfy the lust of his flesh by acting upon the suggestion, commandment or counsel of the Devil, no matter how legitimate the act might seem or how satisfying it might be. That is what Adam had done and in so doing had acted independently of God to satisfy himself. That is what constitutes sin, and sin brings death.

Jesus resisted Satan with the written Word of God. In so doing he defined for us the principle of life: *"Man shall not live by bread alone, but by every word that proceedeth out of the mouth of God."*[53] His life, as a man, was in the word of his Father, not in bread.

Then the Devil took him up into a high mountain, and showed him all the kingdoms of the world in a moment of time:

"All this power will I give thee, and the glory of them: for that is delivered unto me, and to whomsoever I will I give it. If thou, therefore shall worship me, all shall be thine."[54]

Satan's offer was not the kingdoms of the *earth*. He specified the kingdoms of the *world*. There is a difference. The earth was not his to give. The earth is the Lord's, and the fullness thereof.[55] But Satan is the god of this *world*.[56] His dominion has been exercised over this world system ever since its inception when Adam surrendered his authority to the serpent in the Garden of Eden. It was to that incident that Satan referred when he said, ". . . that is delivered unto me, and to whomsoever I will I give it."

The devil showed Jesus all the world's kingdoms, and promised him all the worldly power and glory that man could achieve if he would forsake the will of the Father and pursue this world's fortunes. This is called the lust of the eyes.

Satan was tempting the last Adam as he had tempted the first: with all this power and glory you will no longer be a starving, dying servant of God. You can be like God in this world system.

Jesus responded, *"It is written, thou shalt worship the LORD [Jehovah] thy God, and him <u>only</u> shalt thou serve."*[57]

He was saying submission to any will but the Father's is sin. In reflecting only the will of God, humanity is fulfilling its purpose. That is called righteousness.

Then the devil brought him to Jerusalem and set him on a pinnacle of the temple and said unto him, "If thou be the Son of God, cast thyself down from hence, for it is written, 'He shall give his angels charge over thee to keep thee: and in their hands they shall bear thee up, lest at any time thou dash thy foot against a stone.'"[58]

Satan not only denies the Word of God to tempt man, but sometimes quotes it to deceive him. Here he tempted Jesus, a man, to claim the protection of God's promise while performing a death-defying, self-glorifying act, for his own human advantage. Thus the devil attempted to make God the servant, and man the master.

God is not a servant, protector or assistant to be summoned when man needs help to accomplish his own will. It is not man's prerogative to test God. God is LORD. Man is his servant. Jesus made this clear when he quoted the scripture, *"Thou shall not tempt the Lord thy God."*[59]

Jesus resisted the devil, and emerged from this confrontation victorious over the lust of the flesh, the lust of the eyes, and the pride of life. Where Adam had failed, Jesus succeeded. He believed and obeyed the Father. As a result, the devil departed from him for a season. Having overcome temptation, he returned in the power of the Spirit into Galilee and there went out a fame of him through all the region round about.[60]

Chapter 5 References

1 Romans 5:12
2 Romans 3:10
3 Ecclesiasties 7:20
4 Genesis 5:15
5 I Corinthians 15:21
6 Genesis 4:1-7
7 Genesis 6:1-8
8 Genesis 6:9
9 II Peter 2:5
10 Genesis 22:18; 26:5
11 Genesis 21:12
12 Genesis 25:23
13 Matthew 22:42; John 7:42
14 Isaiah 7:14
15 Micah 5:2
16 Romans 3:19
17 Hebrews 9:22
18 John 1:29
19 I Corinthians 15:45
20 II Corinthians 5:14
21 Isaiah 43:11
22 John 1:1-3
23 John 1:14
24 John 17:4,6
25 John 1:18
26 Luke 9:10
27 I Corinthians 15:21
28 Dr. H.R. DeHaan
29 Isaiah 43:27
30 John 3:16; 1:14

31 Luke 3:38
32 Job 1:6
33 John 1:12
34 Matthew 1:18; Luke 2
35 John 1:18
36 Philippians 2:6-8
37 Hebrews 1:3
38 John 5:19,30
39 II Corinthians 5:19
40 I Corinthians 15:45
41 Romans 5:19
42 Romans 8:3
43 John 6:38
44 Luke 22:42
45 Hebrews 10:7,9
46 Kuke 2:49
47 Matthew 13:55
48 Mark 6:3
49 Hebrews 4:15
50 Matthew 4:1
51 James 1:13
52 Matthew 4:3; Luke 4:3
53 Luke 4:4
54 Luke 4:7
55 I Corinthians 10:26,28
56 II Corinthians 4:4
57 Luke 4:8
58 Luke 4:10
59 Luke 4:11
60 Luke 4:14

God's Eternal Purpose

6
The Reconciling Work

Although he endured the ultimate temptation perpetrated by the ultimate tempter, Jesus endured without blemish. Throughout his entire life he flawlessly performed the father's will and qualified to be the perfect sacrifice for the sins of the rest of us.

Jesus, the Bible says, was made a little lower than the angels "for the suffering of death." He came into the world specifically to taste death for every man.[1]

For hundreds of years before Jesus' birth, men had sacrificed the bodies of bulls and goats to make atonement for their sins. But when Christ came into the world he said to the Father, "Sacrifice and offering thou wouldst not, but a body thou hast prepared for me."[2] Jesus knew from the beginning that his body was prepared by God to be the final sacrifice to pay the penalty for man's sin once for all. Adam, by one act of disobedience had brought death and separation. Now, by one act of obedience, Jesus would remove the barrier that stood between corrupted man and a holy God.[3]

After three years of ministry during which he did immeasurable good, demonstrated righteousness, and performed only God's will, he faced the agony of crucifixion. Jesus had taken up his cross the moment he had been appointed as a sacrifice for sin. Born to be a sacrifice, his human will was constantly and entirely submitted to that of the Father. He was a living sacrifice until the time that his life should be given as a ransom for many.[4] When that time finally came, he stood guiltless before Pilate, falsely indicted for imagined crimes,[5] and condemned to die.

Jesus had already confessed, ". . .for this cause came I unto this hour."[6] So, committing himself to him that judges right-eously, Jesus yielded to the cruel punishment of the cross.[7] There he would die as a sacrificial lamb without spot or blemish. In obedience to the Father's will, as the righteous one he would pay the penalty of the unrighteous. The obedient would suffer for the disobedient, the just for the unjust. He would put away sin by the sacrifice of himself.[8]

The apostle Paul, describing this course of events wrote:

[Christ] *"being in the form of God, thought it not robbery to be equal with God; but made himself of no reputation,* [or, he emptied himself of his divine attributes: he set aside all that was not con-sistent with humanity] *and took upon him the form of a servant, and was made in the likeness of men: and being found in fashion as a man he humbled himself and became obedient unto death, even the death of the cross.*[9] The crucifixion would be the ultimate humiliation.

We read the story and acknowledge the historic facts to be true. But how can we comprehend the magnitude of this sacrifice? The Word of God, equal with the Father, of his own volition becomes flesh to be a servant to God and man. It was a degree of servitude that required death under cruel Roman law, and at the hands of guilty men who deserved to die themselves.

Jesus is the only man who never lived under the authority of the god of this world system. The life of God was evident in him, and Satan hates God. No wonder that the world, over which Satan has dominion, hates Jesus also. Furthermore, Jesus often warned his disciples that the world would hate them as well.[10]

Even today, this hatred is displayed in our modern society, as laws are passed with a view of banishing religion—and specifically Christianity—from every facet of public life. Forms of religion are alive and well, of course, throughout our nation; in corporate board rooms, schools, the military, and every level of government service, but it is not the religion of the Bible. It does not proclaim Jehovah or exalt the name of Jesus Christ.

Eastern religion, the new age, and every humanistic doctrine that exalts man to be like the Most High and denigrates the person of Jesus is acceptable, even where separation of church and state is proclaimed. It is Jesus who is unacceptable today, just as he was in the days of his crucifixion.

At that time Satan, in his fury, conspired to destroy Jesus by provoking the religious leaders to demand his death. But in Satan's passion to destroy Jesus, the man he could not subjugate, he accomplished the Father's will, the sacrifice of the Lamb of God for the sins of the whole world. The apostle Peter would later preach to the men of Israel, *"Jesus of Nazareth, a man approved of God among you. . .him, being delivered by the determinate counsel and foreknowledge of God, you have taken and by wicked hands have crucified and slain."*[11]

Satan is frustrated by the results of his own apparent victory. By the inciting of his people to the destruction of Jesus, he did not destroy his enemy. On the contrary,[12] he caused the sacrifice to be completed, according to the determinate counsel and foreknowledge of God that redeemed those he held captive and destroyed his power over them.[13]

The Scriptures clearly show that Satan is in rebellion against God. His intention is to frustrate God's plan and destroy God's people. However, the scriptures also make clear God's intention that Satan, as an angel, should ultimately render a service to the people of God. Therefore, no matter what hellish thing he does, he only contributes to the advance of God's purpose.[14] This was eminently the case in the death of Jesus.

The Destruction Of Adam's Polluted Race

Paul the apostle wrote, "We thus judge, that if one died for all, *then were all dead."*[15] This is how God sees it too.

Throughout history He has been dealing with only two men. The first was Adam. The second is Christ. As was stated early in this book, God only created one man. The entire human race was cre-

71

ated in him. As part of Adam, his nature is our nature. That's why it's accurate to say, "we were born in sin and shapen in iniquity."[16] That is why "there is none righteous, no not one."[17] It is the reason the apostle Paul said, 'we are *by nature* the children of wrath,'[18] not by our choice or by our actions, but by our *nature*. All who are in Adam are dead in trespasses and sin because that is how we came forth from our father. We bore his fallen image.

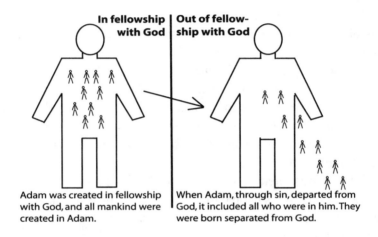

In fellowship with God	Out of fellowship with God
Adam was created in fellowship with God, and all mankind were created in Adam.	When Adam, through sin, departed from God, it included all who were in him. They were born separated from God.

That is the meaning of the scripture that states, ". . .*by the offense of one [man], judgment came upon ALL men to condemnation.*"[19] That also helps us to understand how one man could be the substitute for a whole race. Identifying himself with Adam's race by becoming as Adam had been before he sinned, Jesus is described as the last Adam. Jesus having maintained perfect righteousness, need never die, unless it would be as a substitute for that other man. He could, therefore, pay the death penalty for the victims of Adam's fall. When Jesus would die, then, in God's view, *all would be dead.*

Sin Was Condemned In The Flesh

Sin was the problem in the subhuman race that Adam had spawned. It was to be condemned. Paul wrote, ". . .*God, sending his own Son in the likeness of sinful flesh and [as a sacrifice] for sin condemned sin in the flesh.*"[20] Here's how God dealt with sin. He isolated it, gave it a personality and condemned it *in the flesh.*

We have already seen that Jesus came as Adam had come, as the image of God, with the same potential of sin and death. He faced the same temptations from the same tempter. However, he overcame and lived until his death without one sin upon his record. His *human* nature, therefore, was never a *fallen* nature. He was *the* righteous man. Now he could step forth to become the substitute for the fallen man's sin.[21]

In becoming the sacrifice, he would approach the flaming sword of God's judgment in the very likeness of sinful flesh. That meant that as he had portrayed the image of God in his life, he would now bear in his death the image of fallen Adam. The apostle Paul described it this way, *" He (God) hath made him (Jesus), who knew no sin to be sin for us. . ."*[22] Placed upon the cross, he would assume the identity of Adam's fallen race. He would literally become sin and would prostrate himself, in our place, before the awful judgment of a holy God. And, as sin, he would die.

In the flesh of the Lord Jesus Christ, therefore, sin would be dealt with as a personality and would be condemned once for all. Jesus was considered the last Adam—the terminal man. All of the condemnation meted out upon Adam's sinful race would go with Jesus to the grave. In God's economy, *when one died for all, all died.*[23]

At his trial, Jesus faced the mocking crowd. There he stood, a purple robe draped over his shoulders in mockery, a crown of sharp thorns pressed down upon his head, opening wounds from which blood ran down upon his face. Adding to the absurdity of this bizarre charade, he held in his hand a reed to represent a kingly scepter. And before him, his Roman tormentors fell upon their knees and mocked him, saying, "Hail, King of the Jews!"[24]

How could they know that one day *every* knee would bow before him,[25] and that he would indeed be crowned a king, not only of the Jews, but of all the nations?[26] In fact, he would be called "King of kings, and Lord of lords."[27] Nor could they know that he would then hold in his hand the scepter of righteousness, the authority of his everlasting kingdom, and that every tongue would declare him LORD to the glory of God the Father.[28]

But for now, the crown he wore was the consequence of man's sin. Its thorns had sprung from the accursed earth. The scepter they took from his hand and with which they struck his face was the self-righteousness with which an unbelieving world has smitten the Lamb of God.

As he made his way to his cruel execution at Golgotha, he bore for us the identity of sin. Despised and rejected of men, a man of sorrows and acquainted with grief, he bore our griefs and carried our sorrows—to the cross and to death and to the grave forever.[29]

Darkness fell over the earth, and a cry rang out from the cross, "MY GOD, MY GOD, WHY HAST THOU FORSAKEN ME?"[30] In that terrifying moment "he yielded up the ghost."[31] Jesus surrendered his life in sacrifice for us. The Lamb of God was dead. Sin was judged, and God counted Adam's race as dead. From God's side, the quarrel was over. The last Adam had died. ". . . **we were reconciled to God by the death of his Son."**[32]

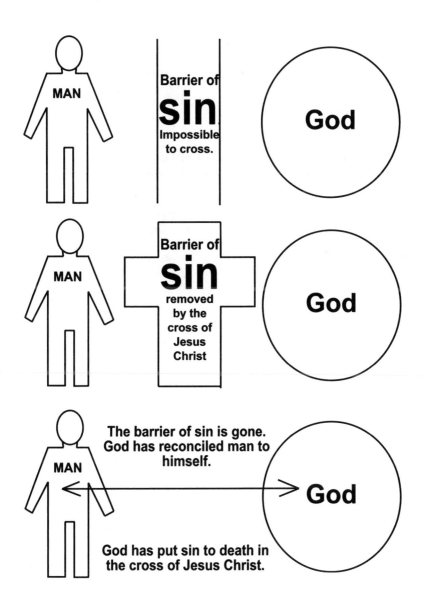

MAN

Barrier of
sin
Impossible to cross.

God

MAN

Barrier of
sin
removed by the cross of Jesus Christ

God

MAN

The barrier of sin is gone. God has reconciled man to himself.

God

God has put sin to death in the cross of Jesus Christ.

Chapter 6 References

1 Hebrews 2:7
2 Hebrews 10:5
3 Hebrews 5:12-21; II Cor.5:19
4 I Timothy 2:6
5 Matthew 26:59; 27:1,2
6 John 18:37; 12:27
7 I Peter 2:23
8 I Pet.3:18; I Tim.2:6; Heb.9:26
9 Philippians 2:6-8
10 John 15:18,24; Mark 13:13
11 Acts 2:22,23
12 Acts 2:23,24
13 Hebrews 2:14
14 Romans 8:28-39
15 II Corinthians 5:14
16 Psalm 51:5
17 Psalm 14:1-3; Romans 3:10-12
18 Ephesians 2:1-3
19 Romans 5:18
20 Romans 8:3b
21 Romans 3:25; John 2:2
22 II Corinthians 5:21
23 II Corinthians 5:14
24 Matthew 27:27-30
25 Romans 14:11
26 Psalm 2
27 Revelation 19:16
28 Philippians 2:11
29 Isaiah 53
30 Matthew 27:46
31 Matthew 27:50
32 Romans 5:10

7
The Second Man

Before Jesus' death, he had taught his disciples many things about himself that they would not understand until after his resurrection. One of these truths was embodied in the parable of the kernel of wheat: *"Except a corn of wheat fall into the ground and die,"* Jesus had said, *"it abides alone; but if it die, it brings forth much fruit."*[1]

Admittedly it is hard to identify the planting of a kernel of wheat with the death and burial of a beloved friend with whom one has walked day and night for a number of years. Planting, for the farmer, is a hopeful season. Death, on the other hand, means grief, despair, disappointment. There is a finality that tends to destroy hope.

"We trusted that it *had been* he which *should have* redeemed Israel. . ." That's what Cleopas was saying as he walked with another of Jesus' disciples after the crucifixion.[2] He was not trusting anymore. All of his blasted hopes were being expressed in the past tense. He had seen the burial of the kernel of wheat, but somehow he could not relate it to the idea of bringing forth much fruit. What he had hoped for through the Messiah was the redeeming of Israel from the Roman oppressors that were occupying his homeland.

But suddenly the gloom of despair and sorrow was shattered.

There, before his very eyes, was Jesus, alive from the dead. Now his hopes were restored and even expanded. There was more to redemption than the deliverance of the nation from Rome's army of occupation. There was deliverance from death.

There were others, too, whose hopes were crushed when Jesus died. One of these was Mary Magdalene. All of her expectations were in this Jesus who had delivered her from the seven demons that had controlled and tormented her body.[3] Now she wept alone outside his empty tomb.[4]

"Mary."

She heard her name. She turned and saw Jesus standing before her, alive from the dead. Moments before, Mary had looked into the empty tomb, despairing because the body of her Lord was gone. Now, suddenly, Mary's world was made bright again. Jesus, her deliverer, had overcome death and the grave. Her deliverance from the power of darkness, then, was greater than she thought. It was not only from sin, but also from death. And it would be forever.

In yet another place, to other despairing disciples, the message came from Jesus' mouth, *"Peace be unto you! Why do thoughts arise in your hearts? Behold my hands and   my feet, that it is I myself: handle me and see: for a spirit hath not flesh and bones as ye see me have. . .these are the words that I spake unto you while I was yet with you. Thus it is written, and thus it behoved Christ to suffer, and to rise from the dead the third day."*[5]

There he stood, alive from the dead and speaking these words to his assembled disciples. They could hardly believe what they saw and heard. Jesus was alive. They had witnessed his death. Now they were witnessing his resurrection. He had overcome sin, and now he had destroyed the power of death. They believed.

In Christ, Death is not Eternal, Life is Eternal.

Today, some would ascribe Jesus' resurrection to their theory of reincarnation, a cycle of life and death, and another life, etc. But the Bible says, "It is appointed unto men *once* to die, and after that the judgment."[6] After death there is judgment and either eternal life with Christ or eternal separation from God from which there is no recourse.

Jesus died once, and God raised him from the dead just as Jesus had prophesied. "Destroy this temple, and in three days I will raise it up again." This he had said concerning the temple of his body.[7] But his disciples had not understood that until they had witnessed his resurrected body.

Jesus cannot die again. According to the scriptures, *"Christ, being raised from the dead, dieth no more. Death hath no more dominion over him."*[8]

The Two Problems Are Resolved

This resurrected Christ, whom the Bible calls "the second man," is the one God had in mind when he looked across the ages of time and said, "Let us make man in our image."[9] In Jesus, the two problems that existed in the garden of Eden – man's PSD and Satan's threatening presence – are resolved. This new race of man is without the potential of sin or death; and Satan, that fallen angel who endeavored to frustrate God's plan for man, has been defeated by him.

The New Testament teaches us that Jesus was begotten twice. That may sound like a surprising new doctrine to some, but it is clearly taught by the apostle Paul. The first time, Jesus was begotten by the Holy Spirit in the womb of the Virgin Mary, who gave birth in the stable at Bethlehem. In that case, Jesus was born to die.

The second time he was begotten, the apostle Paul called him "the first begotten from the dead." As Paul preached to the Jews at Antioch in Pisidia, he told them of the resurrection of Jesus. Referring to the promises God made to the fathers of the nation of Israel, he said, *"God hath fulfilled the same unto us their children, in that he hath raised up Jesus again; as it is also written in the second Psalm, Thou art my Son, this day have I begotten thee."*

Describing Jesus' human birth, the Bible says he was begotten by God. The same term is used to describe his resurrection. The fact that Jesus is 'the *first* begotten from the dead'[10] is significant.

When the Word speaks of his human birth, he is the *only* begotten son. No other son of God was physically begotten of God. But when the Word speaks of Jesus' resurrection, he is the *first* begotten from the dead. In that he is described as the *first*, it is evident that there are others to follow who, in their time, will also be begotten from the dead.[11]

There is a difference between the man that Jesus was in his human birth and the man that he is in his resurrection. When he came into the world through Mary, he came in the likeness of sinful flesh. He was the same kind of man that God had created Adam to be; a man who, because of his ability to choose to disobey, had the potential of sin and death. Jesus had been born to die. And he did die. His life was sacrificed as a ransom for many.

His death reconciled us to God. That is, it took away the barrier of sin that had made it impossible for us to approach God. But, even so, it is his life, not his death, that saves us.[12] Therefore, to be our savior, Jesus must live, and he does. He was begotten again, this time from the dead.

Now there is a difference. He is not like the first Adam had been, his mortal body kept alive by human blood coursing through its veins.[13] He is now an immortal man, alive forevermore by the Spirit of God.[14] He is the *first* begotten from the dead, and all who believe him will be like him when God's temporal plan is finished and his eternal purpose is fulfilled in us.[15]

Having passed through the judgment of the cross and the separation of the grave, Jesus has emerged as the head of a new race, victorious over sin and death. This is who God was seeing when he, in the beginning, looked beyond Adam's race at the second man and said, "Let us make man in our image." Jesus, when confronted with Adam's options, chose to do the Father's will, even to the point of death, beyond which the potential to do otherwise no longer existed.

Jesus, who went to the grave as the last Adam, rose again as the second man, the head of a new creation, the progenitor of a new race called *The New Man.* As we bore the image of Adam, we shall soon bear the perfect image of Christ.[16]

As we read earlier, *"He who knew no sin was made sin for us. . .."* Now hear the rest of that verse: *"that we might be made the righteousness of God in him."*[17] This is the essence of salvation, the truth that seems to evade some who think righteousness is produced by some ability of theirs to perform in a way that will satisfy God.

This is what Curtis (to whom you were introduced in chapter one), and multitudes of others like him need to know. Salvation is of the Lord. When he identified himself with our helpless humanity he became what we were, that we, in him, might be *made* what he is for eternity. It was a glorious trade, if only we will receive it. He was *made* sin for us. We are *made* the righteousness of God in him.

We may not understand all that. Neither did Jesus' disciples. How incredulous they were as he stood before them in his resurrected body. But Jesus made them believe. "Touch me," he said, "a spirit hath not flesh and bones as ye see me have."[18] Then he ate with them. They were to be witnesses that he was alive, even though they had seen him die. That is the heart of the gospel, not man's goodness, nor even man's effort to be good, but the physical resurrection of Jesus and the life he imparts to as many as receive him.

Some are amazed when they hear that Jesus was seen by his disciples for forty days after his resurrection before he ascended to the Father. During that time he taught them of the kingdom of God[19] and promised them power from on high to fulfill the ministry to which he had commissioned them.[20] They were to realize that this indwelling power of the Holy Spirit is the very life of Christ, which would produce in them (and us) the behavior that pleases the Father.

And when he had taught them, they witnessed in one glorious moment his ascension to the Father's right hand,[21] where he has been made both Lord and Christ.[22] Ten days after his ascension, Jesus poured out his Holy Spirit on all flesh, as he had promised. He now indwells those who have believed, delivering them from their sins and making them new creatures in Christ.[23]

CHAPTER 7 References

1. John 12:24
2. Luke 24:13-16
3. Mark 16:9
4. John 20:11-18
5. Luke 24:36-46
6. Hebrew 9:27
7. John 2:19-22
8. Romans 6:9,10
9. Genesis 1:26
10. Revelation 1:5
11. I Corinthians 15:20-23
12. Romans 5:10
13. I Corinthians 15:50
14. I Corinthians 15:46
15. I John 3:1,2
16. I Corinthians 15:42-49
17. II Corinthians 5:21
18. Luke 24:39
19. Acts 1:3
20. Acts 1:8
21. Acts 1:9
22. Acts 2:36
23. II Corinthians 5:17

Chapter

8

Our Part

Perhaps there is one more question that should be asked: *"What must I do to be saved?"* This query takes us back to the initial comments in this book, about relating one's eternal standing to some level of performance and the confidence one *feels.*

New Testament writers addressed what could be considered our part in God's plan to make man in his image. The apostle Paul preached *repentance* toward God, and *faith* toward the Lord Jesus Christ.[1] Those two elements, *repentance* and *faith,* were his theme.

In describing Adam's fall, we used these terms, Adam *repented* of submission to God's authority, and put his *faith* in Satan's lie. In that model it was very evident what repentance involved. Adam changed his mind. Whereas formerly he had honored God's authority, suddenly he repented. He joined Satan in doubting God's integrity. Figuratively he turned around. He turned his back upon God, and his face toward the tempter. That's repentance *from* God.

Secondly, he trusted Satan's words. He believed he wouldn't die but would be like God. His faith was *toward* Satan, with the consequence that he obeyed the lie. His unrighteous act of disobedience to God resulted in death. We, then, individually inherited that relationship quite apart from anything we did ourselves.

The case of Jesus, the second man was different. He did not turn from God and did not believe the lie. He obeyed God and accomplished everything necessary to save the fallen members of Adam's race.[2]

The voices of the prophets and apostles echo down through the corridors of history, calling men of Adam's race to repent. John the Baptist said, "Repent, for the Kingdom of God is at hand."[3] Jesus came, saying, "Repent, for the kingdom of God is at hand."[4] Peter and Paul came with the message of repentance also. They all meant, "Change your mind. Turn around. Agree with God."

Authority is the issue, as it has always been. Will we submit to the rightful authority of Jehovah, the author of the universe? Or will it be the usurped authority of Lucifer, the god of this world system? True repentance turns us from all others to acknowledge the authority of God.

To the message of "Repentance toward God," the apostle Paul added, "and faith toward the Lord Jesus Christ." The Bible says, "Without faith, it is impossible to please God."[5] Faith is not merely a positive mental attitude toward something one has set one's mind upon. Saving faith is trust focused on the person of the Lord Jesus Christ. It is the unshakable confidence that his redeeming work fully satisfies the righteous demands of God's justice on our behalf.

Savior Of All Men

As a young believer I came upon the text, "we trust in the living God, who is the savior of *all* men, *specially* of those that believe."[6] I pondered that. In the light of many Bible verses that spoke of eternal judgment,[7] the Lake of Fire,[8] etc., the idea of all men being saved seemed incongruous. And that phrase, "specially of those that believe"—did that mean some are more saved than others? I had to put the questions on the back burner, so to speak, to ponder some other time when I would understand a little more.

It is clear to me now that Jesus is the only Savior there is. He is the Savior of every member of Adam's race. Any person who spends eternity in the Lake of Fire will do so in spite of the fact that he had a savior.[9] Jesus is the savior of *all* men. But especially of those that believe, because those who believe will enjoy the benefits of that salvation for all eternity.

In Acts 16 there is the story of the apostle Paul, with his partner, Silas, in jail at Philippi, a Roman city in Macedonia. They had apparently spoken of God to the jailer in charge. In their darkened cell, as midnight approached, they sang praises to God, which perhaps helped persuade all who heard them that they were his messengers. But nothing to that point had been so convincing as the earthquake that suddenly rocked the jail. Fear gripped the jailer's heart. Terrified and humbled, this broken man fell down at the apostles' feet and cried out, "Sirs, what must I do to be saved?"[10]

Paul responded, "Believe on the Lord Jesus Christ and thou shalt be saved."[11]

Specific Things To Believe

Many have taken these eleven little words as their abbreviated gospel, giving the impression that simply believing in the existence of Jesus constitutes salvation. Perhaps they did not notice that Paul then "spake unto him the word of the Lord, and to all that were in his house."

There were specific things to believe. The words, "Believe on the Lord Jesus Christ and thou shalt be saved...." were spoken to a man full of repentance, willing to forsake his life, and crying out from a desperate heart, "What must I do to be saved?" To other men, with other frames of mind, Paul spoke other words. But even to the jailer, Paul spoke the Word of the Lord, adding to his understanding the specifics that he and his family must believe about Jesus.

Compare Paul's message to the one often heard in our contemporary world. Paul preached, "If thou shalt confess with thy mouth the Lord Jesus [or Jesus as Lord], and shalt believe in thine heart that God hath *raised him from the dead* thou shalt be saved." [12] Today that message has been translated into: "If you will confess Jesus as your *savior,* and believe that he *died* on the cross, you will be saved."

Is there a difference? Of course there is. And the difference is significant. The key words in Paul's message are *"Lord"* and *"raised from the dead."* Compared to *"Savior"* and *"died"* in the

85

contemporary message.

First of all, Lord (Gr. Kurios) means supreme in authority, controller. It is conceivable, however, that one might be a savior and command no authority at all. There is a significant difference, therefore, between calling Jesus savior and acknowledging him as Lord. Jesus himself made clear his own definition of Lord when he said, "Why call ye me Lord, Lord, and do not the things that I say?"[13]

Secondly, Jesus' resurrection is the central theme of every recorded salvation message preached by the apostles. It is that fact we must believe to be saved. In his death Jesus brought Adam's race to an end. He put us to death, thereby settling sin's account forever. But if that were the end of the story, it would be the end of us. If the message stopped there, it would be *bad* news, not the gospel (good news). Paul preached, "if you...believe in your heart that God has *raised him from the dead*, you shall be saved."

These two facts, *Jesus is Lord* and *God has raised him from the dead,* combine to define for us what and who Jesus is now and what our relationship to him must be. He is not a figure of ancient history, a dead savior of a bygone era. He is a presently living Lord, seated at the Father's right hand with all power (authority) in heaven and in earth,[14] who has purchased us to himself by his own blood.[15] That is what we must acknowledge to be saved.

Amazingly, there are some who resist this message of the apostles and of Jesus, saying that repentance constitutes works and that acknowledging Jesus to be Lord is an optional second step. They would say that simply believing the facts of Jesus death, life and resurrection constitutes salvation. People forget that even the devils believe those things and tremble.[16]

Jesus made it plain that there will be those who will say, "Lord, Lord, have we not prophesied in thy name? and in thy name have cast out devils? And in thy name done many wonderful works? And then will [Jesus] profess unto them, I never knew you: depart from me, ye that work iniquity."[17]

Perhaps that explains why there are so many professing Christians whose lifestyles and philosophies so closely parallel those of the world; and why so many do not experience what it means to be saved *from their sins.*[18]

It was repenting *from* God's truth and believing Satan's lie that brought Adam under the absolute power of the god of this world. That authority, working in all of Adam's offspring, produced the unmistakable evidence of sin in the character, philosophy, and behavior of them all.

Through repentance *toward* God and by believing the truth of Jesus, we are set free from the dominion of sin[19] and as children of God are established in the authority of the resurrected Lord. That authority, working in the believers who have become sons of God, will, in time, produce the unmistakable evidence of the righteousness of Christ in their character, philosophy and behavior.[20]

Jesus Is Lord

Some fear the demand that, to be saved one must confess Jesus Christ as Lord. They interpret that to mean that absolute, continual submission to his authority, without deviation, must be displayed before one can be saved. None of the apostles suggested that perfection in behavior was required to produce salvation, or that it was the automatic and instant result. If such were the case, they would not have spent time instructing saved people what to do in the event that they sinned,[21] or rebuking them for the apparent ungodly actions that were frequently on display among the believers.[22]

Confessing Jesus as Lord has to do with what he is, not what I am. It is a confession that I have ceased to see myself as the authority over my own life. I have recognized as sin my independence from his Word and rebellion against his rightful authority. I am ready to say I am relinquishing my imagined rights. It is not a matter of saying I have attained perfect submission, and the degree of my obedience is such that I am proving my worth to be saved.

Confession of Jesus' Lordship is only the beginning, but until I confess that, I will feel little constraint to submit to his authority. In fact, until I am ready to confess him as Lord, I am not ready to be saved. I have not repented.

Resurrection

Can you imagine the indescribable joy, elation and hope that filled the disciples who were still mourning Jesus' death, when suddenly he stood before them alive? Here was tangible evidence that Jesus had conquered death, the most dreadful of all enemies. The grave, obviously, could not hold him.

This is how the gospel began. What they were believing at that moment was not a doctrinal statement about some benign historic event. They were partakers in the drama of resurrection and eternal life without the potential of sinning or dying any more. It was this risen Jesus who told them specifically that all power had been given to him in heaven and in earth. He was Lord and Christ.[23] These were the facts of which they were witnesses, and this was the message the Lord told them to preach. Anything less is not the gospel.

CHAPTER 8 References
1. Acts 20:21
2. John 8:29; Hebrews 5:8,9
3. Mark 1:3,4
4. Mark 1:15
5. Hebrews 11:6
6. I Timothy 4:10
7. Matthew 25:26
8. Revelation 21:8
9. John 3:14–21,26
10. Acts 16:25–34
11. Acts 16:31
12. Romans 10:9,10
13. Luke 6:46
14. Matthew 28:18
15. Acts 20:28
16. James 2:19
17. Matthew 7:21–23
18. Matthew 1:21
19. Romans 6:7,14
20. Matthew 7:16–20
21. I John 1:9; 2:1
22. I Corinthians 5
23. Acts 2:36

Chapter

9

Firstfruits

One day, while traveling across the Canadian prairies, I accompanied a friend on a tour of his wheat fields. Almost as far as the eye could see the wheat rippled like some golden sea as the wind passed over it. From time to time, as we drove around the perimeters of the fields, my friend would stop, wade out into the waving grain, and gather a handful of wheat. By inspecting those handfuls he was able to evaluate his coming harvest. It was his knowledgeable assumption that those "first fruits" he had plucked accurately represented the condition of the whole crop. He could be reasonably sure that the rest of the harvest would be the same as the "first fruits."

The scriptures make it clear that the believers' hope is resurrection from the dead. Jesus and all the apostles compared that resurrection to a great harvest. The apostle Paul described Jesus as the firstfruits of that resurrection harvest: *"But now is Christ risen from the dead, and become the firstfruits of them that slept. For since by man came death, by man came also the resurrection of the dead. For as in Adam all die, even so in Christ shall all be made alive. But every man in his own order: Christ the firstfruits; afterward they that are Christ's at his coming."*[1]

When the apostle Paul wrote this verse he was probably thinking of one of Israel's traditional feasts, prescribed in the law of the Old Testament. There were several feasts which came at logical times throughout the year, commemorating specific historical events, or as the case of the Feast of Firstfruits, to celebrate the coming harvest. Israel's feasts, however, had dual significance; they were not only commemorative, but also prophetic. Each one represented an aspect of the career of the expected Messiah.

The first feast of the year was the Passover, followed by the Feast of Firstfruits, the Feast of Weeks, the Feast of Trumpets, and finally the Feast of Tabernacles.[2] All of them signified various aspects of the life and ministry of the Lord Jesus: his death, his resurrection, the outpouring of his Holy Spirit, his return, and his coming kingdom.

The Passover, historically, commemorated Israel's deliverance from Egyptian slavery.[3] At that time, an unblemished lamb was slain by each family and the blood painted on the door posts of their houses. God sent his destroying angel to judge Egypt, bringing death to every firstborn in every home, except where the blood was applied. God had promised his people, "When I see the blood I will pass over you."[4] Hence the name *Passover*. But the Passover also looked ahead, signifying the future death of the coming Messiah, the lamb of God whose blood would be shed to deliver them (and us) from the judgment of God.[5]

The Feast of Firstfruits, celebrated just before the harvest was to begin, was a sequel to the Passover feast, typifying the resurrection of the Lord Jesus. In the tradition of this feast, when the wheat harvest was ready, the priest waded into the waving grain and with his sickle chopped the first sheaf, the firstfruits of the harvest. On the first day after the Sabbath, he lifted it heavenward and waved it before the LORD as an offering to be accepted for all the people.[6]

As we read the New Testament account of Jesus' resurrection, the significance is clear. Jesus Christ is represented by both the priest and the sheaf. The Lord Jesus, as our priest, offered himself before the Father to be accepted for us. It was appropriate that the priest in the Old Testament should perform his ceremony on the day after the Sabbath, the first day of the week, for it was then that the Lord Jesus would be raised from the tomb to present himself on our behalf alive from the dead.[7] But the picture doesn't stop there. In a most wonderful climax to it all, the entire harvest was gathered in, each shock of grain being exactly as the firstfruits. Jesus is the kernel of wheat that fell into the ground and died, spoken of in John 12:24,25. And we are the fruit that he brought forth in the same image. He is also the firstfruits of the resurrection harvest. All the redeemed are the harvest which is to follow. To the harvester, all the harvest will be as the firstfruits. The life that is in Christ is the same life that is in all who are in him.[8]

The likeness of the harvest to the grain that was planted is not the result of any human skill. It is an act of God. The forces of nature which God has set in motion are at work at every stage, ultimately to bring about that perfect likeness. A most remarkable promise in God's word says precisely that about the resurrection harvest: *"All things work together for good to them that love God, to them who are the called according to his purpose. For whom he did foreknow, he also did predestinate to be conformed to the image of his son, that he might be the firstborn among many brethren. Moreover, whom he did predestinate, them he also called: and whom he called, them he also justified: and whom he justified, them he also glorified."*[9]

As all who are in Adam share his nature and his condemnation, so all who are in Christ are partakers of his divine nature [10] and his righteous life. There is no condemnation to those who are in him.[11] In fact, the scriptures yield another sure promise which cannot fail: "As is the earthy, such are they also that are earthy: and as is the heavenly such are they also that are heavenly. And as we have borne the image of the earthy, we shall also bear the image of the heavenly."[12]

At the resurrection, the perfect image of God will be fully realized in those who are in Christ, as it is in him who is the firstfruits of that glorious harvest.[13]

CHAPTER 9 References
1. I Corinthians 15:20-23
2. Leviticus 23
3. Exodus 12
4. Exodus 12:13
5. I Corinthians 5:7
6. Leviticus 23:9-11
7. John 20:1,17
8. Colossians 1:27
9. Romans 8:28-30
10. II Peter 1:4
11. Romans 8:1-4
12. I Corinthians 15:48-49
13. I John 3:1-3

Chapter
10
The New Man

We have looked at the first man, Adam, and seen his failings. We understand how he produced a race of fallen humanity which, at best, was something less than human when measured by God's rule.

We have looked at the second man, Jesus, and seen his victories over temptation, sin and death. We understand that he was humanity as God meant it to be. Always doing only the will of the Father, he was the express image of God. "In him dwelt the fullness of the Godhead bodily."

We understand how, through the sacrifice of himself, he put sin and the sinner to death and through his resurrection has become the head of a new and potentially perfect race of humanity. Conversion from being mere members of Adam's dead race to being alive in Christ has made us *the New Man*. That's the term Paul uses to describe the believers collectively.[1]

In this transition from the *first* man to the *new* man (which Jesus called being born again),[2] we have entered into the process of becoming conformed to the image of Christ, who is the express image of God. One day, the process will end, "and we shall be like him, for we shall see him as he is." On that day, God's temporal plan for us will end, and we will be introduced to his eternal purpose.

Meanwhile, how are we to live? What are we to understand of the principles that govern us in Christ? We were citizens of this world. Now, in Christ, we are citizens of heaven.[3] We were sons of Adam, but no longer. Now we are sons of God.[4] Obviously, everything has changed. The scripture says:

"Therefore, if any man be in Christ he is a new creature: old things are passed away; behold, all things are become new. And all things are of God, who hath reconciled us to himself by Jesus Christ. . . "[5]

Jesus was, above all, the sacrifice for our sins. But he was also our example.[6] In Jesus' earthly life we have an example of the relationship, attitudes and conduct that glorify the Father. From our new birth to the time we die, or are caught up to meet Christ, we should measure ourselves by his example.

People often ask, What is going to happen to us in eternity? or What kind of bodies will we have after the resurrection? or What will we do in heaven? Although we may not have all the answers to our questions, God has answered them in the person of Christ. If we want to see God's ideal for us, it is displayed in Jesus. If we want to know what we will be like, we can look at him. From his birth to his death, he was, by God's standard, the norm of what man should be.

Christ was born of the flesh, and of the Spirit at the same time. We also were born of the flesh, and we were born of the Spirit when we trusted Christ. He lived a natural life with its trials and temptations; we are doing that now. He died a physical death; so will we, unless Jesus should come first. He arose physically from the grave in a resurrected body; so will we.[7] He was caught up to be with the Father; we also will be caught up at his coming.[8] When he comes again, he will rule on the earth for a thousand years; so will we, because we are to reign with him.[9]

This is why, as we have already seen, Jesus is called the firstfruits. But, even so, we are not little replicas of Jesus, able to function independently of him, any more than he could function independently of the Father. That, remember, is what Adam had been tempted to do and had introduced sin and death as a result.

Jesus is the unique son of God, the head of the new race, of which we are a part, even as Adam was the head of the race of which we *were* a part. As it was Adam's life in us then, that continually offended God's righteousness, it is Jesus' life in us now that pleases the Father. Apart from him we are nothing.

God Works In Us

In Jesus we can see the demonstration of this principle of life. Jesus lived his divine life in a mortal body. In that human flesh, with which every person can identify, God lived.

It was difficult for Philip, one of Jesus' disciples, to comprehend what Jesus meant when he said, *"I am the Way, the Truth, and the Life: no man cometh unto the Father but by me. If you had known me, ye should have known my Father also: and from henceforth ye know him, and have seen him."*

Philip said unto him, "Lord, show us the Father, and it sufficeth us."

Jesus said unto him, "Have I been so long time with you, and have you not known me Philip? He that hath seen me hath seen the Father; and how sayest thou then, show us the Father?"[10]

Some may have assumed, from this portion of scripture, that the Father and the Son are the same. That was not Jesus' point. His next words were to reveal the principle of life at work in his mortal body: "but the Father that dwelleth in me, *he doeth the works."*

The Father is an eternal, immortal Spirit. Jesus was a mortal man. According to Jesus, his own humanity, apart from the Father, was as helpless as yours.[11] Didn't he say, "The Son can do nothing of himself" and again, "Of my own self I can do nothing."? But even after saying that, he went about doing everything: restoring sight to the blind, raising the dead, walking on water. Jesus did it all. How?

"The Father that dwelleth in me," Jesus said, "he doeth the works."

From the beginning of his mortal life in the manger at Bethlehem, Jesus had been committed to the will of his Father. As a consequence, he, as a man, was a vessel in which the Father was on display. No wonder Jesus was able to say, "If you have seen me, you have seen the Father," not the Father's form but his nature, his character and his behavior.

"No man hath seen God (The Father) at any time; the only begotten Son, which is in the bosom of the Father, he hath declared [fully revealed] him."[12]

Jesus Lived By The Father; We Are To Live By Jesus

Perhaps Philip did not understand everything Jesus meant when he said, "If you have seen me you have seen the Father." But it is likely he understood even less when Jesus said, *"Verily, verily, I say unto you, he that believeth on me, the works that I do shall he do also; and greater works than these shall he do: because I go unto my Father."*[13]

Because of this verse, many have attempted to imitate what Jesus did in the Gospels, thinking we should be able to do those and even greater works. But what is greater than raising Lazarus from the dead? or feeding the multitudes? or walking on water? or giving sight to the blind? As the saying goes, those are hard acts to follow.

To be sure, there are those who advertise miracles and mighty works. But when the dust has settled and the drum rolls have faded away, the results are no greater than for those who quietly believe the promises of God and with patience wait for them. It is God who works in us both to will and to do of his good pleasure.[14]

Listen again to Jesus' words. *"he that believeth on me, the works that I—do—shall he do also."* The tense of the verb is the key to understanding Jesus' promise. He did not say "the things that I *have done*," or "that I *did*." He said, "the works that I *do*!" (Only one major modern version of the Bible erroneously translates this in the past perfect tense. If you use that version, it would be perfectly acceptable to make a note to yourself in the margin.) Jesus was doing each day whatever the Father was doing, nothing else. And Jesus made it clear that the Father dwelling in him was doing his own work.

Now Jesus is saying, in those who believe on him this same relationship will occur. The works that Jesus is doing *today, here,* he will do through those who believe. Not all that Jesus does to-day will be duplicates of what he did then. He can do spectacular and miraculous works, but not all that Jesus does would fit that description. We are not to try to duplicate the works that he *did*. We are to be available vessels that he might manifest in us what he is doing now.

This is the principle of Christian life—Christ working in us:

"For it is God that worketh in you, both to will and to do of his good pleasure."[14]

"Christ in you, the hope of glory."[15]

"Abide in me, and I in you. As the branch cannot bear fruit of itself, except it abide in the vine; no more can ye, except ye abide in me. I am the vine, ye are the branches: he that abideth in me, and I in him, the same bringeth forth much fruit: for without me ye can do nothing."[16]

But Jesus also said, "and greater works than these shall ye do, because I go unto my Father." What did he mean by that? Are we to do something greater than raising Lazarus, and walking on water?

Qualitatively there are no greater works than those that Jesus did. He manifested every aspect of the Father's name to the men whom God gave him out of the world.[17] Now, as the body of Christ, those who are saved are to manifest him to the entire world.

In Jesus' day the body of Christ was Jesus' body, geographically limited to the nation to which he had come and in which he lived and died. But now the body of Christ comprises those in whom he dwells, filling the world's nations with the manifest life of Christ. The "greater works" are quantitative. What Jesus is doing he will do simultaneously around the world through those in whom he dwells and works.

The Old Testament prophets had forecast the coming of the man who would be the revelation of Jehovah to his people. He would open the way, delivering them from their bondage to sin into the glorious liberty of the kingdom of God. Jesus fulfilled those prophecies. He demonstrated God's version of humanity and loosed those who were bound in Adam's world. As well as being our Savior, he became our example, in attitude and relationship to the Father, to people, to circumstances and to life.

Jesus: Humanity In The Kingdom Of God

"The Spirit of the Lord is upon me, because he hath anointed me to preach the Gospel to the poor; he hath sent me to heal the broken hearted, to preach deliverance to the captives, and recovering of sight to the blind, to set at liberty them that are bruised, to preach the acceptable year of the Lord.[18]

The power in Jesus' life was the result od who he is. The example he has given us is that power is not the result of simply experiencing the Spirit coming upon him. The power resulted from resisting the tempter through the Spirit.[19] Adam, too, had enjoyed fellowship with the Father and the presence and life of the Spirit. He had been crowned with glory and honor. But he did not resist the tempter. He did not return from his encounter in the power of the Spirit but rather in defeat and disgrace. Spiritual power in the life of God's Son (or sons) is the result of walking after the Spirit, and resisting the tempter by the power of the Spirit.

During Jesus' temptation in the wilderness he had resisted the lust of the flesh, the lust of the eye, and the pride of life. Each time he had prevailed by using the Word of God.

Today, there is much made of spiritual experiences but too little said about living by every word of God, worshipping the Lord God, and serving him only, or not tempting God by using his Word for our own ends. It is an eternal truth that we cannot serve two masters. No matter what kind of spiritual experience we may have once enjoyed, spiritual power in daily life is the result of subordinating the propensities of our flesh to the leading of the Spirit.[20]

Jesus Was Anointed To Preach The Gospel To The Poor

Until the time of his anointing, there is no record that Jesus had preached anything. He had lived through infancy, childhood, puberty, adolescence, and manhood, in trade and possibly business, at all times and in all circumstances, constantly going about the Father's business. Finally, being tried in a face to face confrontation with Satan himself, Jesus had, in his helpless humanity, rested on the unchanging word of God and had prevailed. He was ready now.

He had returned from that conflict in the power of the Spirit.

The poor, the downtrodden, the underprivileged heirs of Adam's corrupt nature were to hear now from Jesus' lips the good news of the gospel—man had overcome sin.

"He Hath Sent Me To Heal The Broken Hearted. "[21]

Despair must have wrung the hearts of Adam and Eve when they realized the ugliness of naked flesh for the first time. Before their fall they had been crowned with glory and honor. When they had looked upon each other they had seen the glory and the image of God. No longer. The sudden realization of sin's enormous consequence was staggering. They were paralyzed by the fear of God's displeasure. And as time went by, Eve's heart must have broken when her son, Cain, through jealousy and hatred, spilled the blood of his brother, Abel.[22]

Every wretched generation of Adam's offspring saw the consequences of his one act of disobedience—the rape, destruction and death of their children. The word *brokenhearted,* as used in this verse, comes from a root that conjures up the image of grapes being crushed in a winepress;[23] broken or maimed like a lamb torn by a marauding lion, an offering made unacceptable to God.

Under the cruel dominion of Satan, man has been subject to this abuse, unable to rise above the heartfelt sorrow that crushes the souls of Adam's seed. But now there was a man who had torn the lion and broken the winepress; one who had come as a perfect offering, with a life acceptable to God; one not marred by submission to sin. In Jesus there was healing for the broken hearted.

"To Preach Deliverance To The Captives"

When God had commissioned his first man, Adam, he had given him authority over the works of his hands. Therefore, he had power even over the serpent. Even the fallen angels were the works of God's hands. Satan had no power over the man except that which Adam himself was willing to give him. God was Lord, and under him the man ruled. But, as we already know, Adam, through unbelief of God's Word and confidence in Satan's lie, yielded to captivity. Now spiritually dead, his will was dominated by Satan.

No matter how free they were externally, Adam's descendants

would always be dominated internally by the prince of darkness. They were born captive in an inner dungeon from which they could never escape. The desire for inward peace would drive them to external frenzy—and in the end to frustration and despair. Satan held the key to this inner prison that forever precluded freedom for Adam's race. There is no peace for the wicked.[24]

But now the last Adam had come. This man, Jesus, had faced the warden of the world, had retained God's authority, and kept the keys of his inner man. He had triumphed where the first Adam had surrendered. Now the keys were in his hand to set the captives free.[25]

No matter how high the prison walls nor how strong the iron gates that hold the outward man; no matter how cruel the cross that crucifies the body, now there is freedom within. No restraints limit the new man from soaring to the heavenlies. No dungeon is deep enough or dark enough to hold captive the spirit of those who have been made to sit together in heavenly places in Christ.[26]

"The Recovering Of Sight To The Blind"

Not only had man been made poor by sin; not only had he experienced the emotional trauma of a broken heart and the frustration of spiritual imprisonment: he had also been blinded by the god of this world [27]. He could no longer see God as Adam had seen him through the eyes of a living spirit. Adam, having partaken of the forbidden fruit, found himself with a knowledge of good and evil but without power to do good. In gaining the power to know good and evil, he had lost the ability to discern God.

His descendants were painfully aware of the despotic and tyrannical overlord of this world system, but they could no longer "see" God, nor discern his will. Their spiritual eyes were blind; they lived in a world of unending darkness, full of problems without solutions.

But now Jesus had come. He had not surrendered to the god of this world. His eyes were still open to the kingdom of God. He could "see" what the Father was doing and was able to do likewise.[28] With no blindness to cloud his vision, he could see clearly to do the Father's will and to restore the sight of those who had been made blind. Men and women who had not seen God since the fall of Adam were suddenly confronted with his express image. By looking at Jesus, they could see the Father. And by hearing his word, they could know the Father's will.

"To Set At Liberty Them That Are Bruised"

The bruises inflicted by sin are many. The halt, the maimed, the sick and dying, wounded in spirit and in body, lie in pitiful array along the pathway of life. Jesus saw them there. For thirty-eight years one crippled man lay beside the pool of Bethesda.[29] No helper and no self effort could gain his recovery. But one day Jesus' word came, "Arise, take up thy bed and walk." He rose and walked.

In Cana, Jesus spoke the word, "Go thy way, thy son liveth." And the nobleman's son in Capernaum, twenty five miles away, began to recover from his sickness.[30] The blind, halt, maimed, the leprous, and even the dead, experienced the liberation of Jesus' healing words. No consequence of sin could stand before the liberating force of Jesus' presence.

"And To Preach The Acceptable Year Of The Lord"

Jesus did not come into the world by accident. His birth didn't occur at some random time or place. There was a schedule. This miraculously born son of a Jewish virgin was wrapped in swaddling clothes and laid gently in Bethlehem's manger exactly on time.

The Bible states, *"When the fullness of the time was come, God sent forth his son, made of a woman..."*[31]. For centuries the prophets had foretold the coming of the Lord Jesus. From Moses to Malachi, all had testified of him. Exactly on schedule, he arrived.

"The hour is coming," Jesus said to the Pharisees at Jerusalem, *"and now is, when the dead shall hear the voice of the Son of God, and they that hear shall live."*[32] This is a reference to those who, although dead in trespasses and sin, hear his voice and live, being born again by the Spirit of God.

He followed this by saying, *"The hour is coming* [but not yet] *in the which all that are in the graves shall hear his voice, and shall come forth..."* This is a reference to the resurrection day, to which we look forward with eager hope.

At Jesus' first appearance, the time had come for Adam's race, dead in trespasses and sin, to hear his life-giving voice. Jesus came preaching that the kingdom of God was at hand. Today is the day of salvation; now is the accepted time. Jesus was declaring the acceptable year of the Lord.

Yet to come is the day when he will return with a trumpet sound, when even those in the grave shall hear his voice and come forth.

CHAPTER 10 References

1. Ephesians 2:15
2. John 3:3
3. Philippians 3:20; John 17:14-16
4. John 1:12; Romans 8:16
5. II Corinthians 5:17,18
6. I Peter 2:21
7. I Corinthians 15:49-53
8. I Thesselonians 4:16,17
9. Revelation 5:9
10. John 14:5-9
11. John 5:19,30
12. John 1:18
13. John 14:12
14. Philippians 2:13
15. Colossians 1:27
16. John 15:4,5
17. John 17:6
18. Luke 4:18,19
19. Luke 4:1-14
20. Galatians 5:16
21. Luke 4:18
22. Genesis 4:8
23. Lament. 1:14,15
24. Isaiah 57:21
25. Colossians 1:13
26. Ephesians 2:6
27. II Corinthians. 4:4
28. John 5:19,20
29. John 5:1-9
30. John 4:46-53
31. Galatians 4:4
32. John 5:25

Dominion Over the World

After Jesus' baptism and anointing by the Holy Spirit, he withstood the tempter and returned to Nazareth in the power of the Spirit. He taught in the synagogue at Nazareth, declaring himself to be the anointed one of whom Isaiah had prophesied. The people who heard him were infuriated to the point of murder. But, as badly as they wanted to kill him, he went his way, and they could do nothing to him.[1]

The scene was one of hatred, violence and confusion. Jesus was like an intruder in a bee hive. He was *in* the world, but not *of* it. He was the only human being not under the dominion of this world's god. Jesus was standing upon the earth, within the boundaries of Satan's rule, but entirely exempt from it. He was a hated intruder into the kingdom of darkness. Like bees protecting their hive, the world's leaders were violent with rage.

Jesus was in the world but not of it. He was still in heavenly places because he was under the Father's authority.

Power Over Demons, The Rulers Of This World

"And in the synagogue there was a man that had a spirit of an unclean devil and cried out with a loud voice, saying, 'Let us alone. What have we to do with thee, thou Jesus of Nazareth? Art thou come to destroy us? I know thee who thou art, the holy one of God.' And Jesus rebuked him, saying, 'Hold thy peace and come out of him.' And when the devil had thrown him in the midst, he came out of him, and hurt him not. They were all amazed and spoke among themselves, saying, 'What a word is this! for with authority and power he commandeth the unclean spirits, and they come out.'"[2]

No one had ever seen a man like this before because no one had ever seen a man in his unfallen state; one who had not surrendered to the dominion of the world. Hope was kindled in men and women who longed to be free from the bondage of the world system.

Jesus simply took dominion over every consequence of the fall. Fevers were dispelled, sicknesses healed, and devils were cast out. People who knew nothing but bondage were seeing humanity as God had made it, the image in which Adam had been created.

"And the people sought him, and came unto him, and stayed [restrained] *him, that he should not depart from them."[3]*

Preaching The Kingdom Of God

" And he said unto them, 'I must preach the Kingdom of God in other cities, for thereunto am I sent'." [4]

He didn't preach as others had. He spoke irresistible words of truth, with a grace and authority, which proceeded from a life such as none had ever seen before. His preaching was powerful. The life gave credibility to the words. For this reason the people pressed upon him to hear the word of God. In one instance:

As he stood by the Lake of Gennesaret, there were two ships standing by the lake, but the fishermen were gone out of them, washing their nets. He entered into one of the ships which belonged to Simon, and asked him to push out a little from the *land. Then Jesus sat down and taught the people from the ship.*[5]

Wherever people assembled, there Jesus ministered words of life to them. They realized that he cared for them because he involved himself in their lives. He still does. That has never changed.

When he finished speaking he said to Simon, "Launch out into the deep, and let down your nets for a draft." And Simon answered him, "Master, we have worked all night and have taken nothing! Nevertheless at your word I will let down the net."

When they had done this they caught "a great multitude" of fish, and their net broke. They called their partners who were in the other ship to come and help them, and they filled both ships until they began to sink.

Simon Peter fell down at Jesus' knees, saying, "Depart from me, for I am a sinful man, O Lord." for he and his partners were astonished at the catch of fish which they had taken. And Jesus said to Simon, "Fear not, from henceforth you shall catch men."[6]

Principles Of The Kingdom Of God
Jesus not only preached the kingdom of God, he demonstrated it. These men earned their bread by the sweat of their faces. Sometimes they labored all night in vain. Since Adam sinned, the principle of "sweat to eat" prevailed. It took hard work and all of one's time just to survive.[7]

But in the kingdom of God it wasn't so. For Adam, from the beginning, there had been important work to do. He was to dress and keep the Garden of Eden. It is evident that energy, industry, diligence and productivity are words befitting the Kingdom of God. God has ordained us to work and has even instructed us that those who will not work should not eat.[8] But our work is not for mere survival's sake.

In Adam's case, God had supplied abundantly for every requirement of his sustenance. Adam's work before the fall was simply the diligent performance of God's revealed will. There were no shortages or failures. There was no grumbling or slackness, just an eager pursuit of God's revealed will.

What had changed all that was not Adam's unwillingness to work. It was his unbelief, his unwillingness to trust God.

Jesus, now, was demonstrating afresh the principles of life in God's kingdom before the multitudes who watched him and followed him about. He had no possessions. No ambitions pressed their demands upon him. He never disobeyed the Father or experienced the curse of rebellion or independance. His Father was his provider and his Father's will was his occupation. Had he not said, "Man shall not live by bread alone, but by every word of God?"[9]

Simon Peter and his partners had labored all night and had caught nothing. Their living depended on their catch, and unfortunately, this had been a bad day. But here is Jesus, sitting in their boat, worrying not in the least about food or drink, but spending his time teaching the people the word of God.

Now Jesus speaks the Father's words, "Let down your nets for a draft." When they obeyed that word they were astonished at the results: a draft of fish such as they had never seen before. All night long, directed by their own experience and knowledge, they had cast their nets for try after try, but not once for a draft of fish.

When Jesus spoke, however, he did not suggest another *try*, he told them to let down their nets *for a draft*. In his command was a promise of success. That, also, has not changed. As they did, we also can have the confidence to obey his commands and stand upon his word.

They did according to his word, and he did according to his promise. Now they *saw* the kingdom of God of which they had *heard* in the preaching of Jesus. Last night they had fished independently of any command from God. Today they had fished *according to* God's command. What a difference! All the familiar movements were the same, but the results were incomparable. Acting under his authority, they experienced the fulfillment of his word. They were experiencing life in the Kingdom of God.

Jesus had said, "Fear not." There was no need to live by the old priorities, to neglect everything else just to keep food on their table and clothes on their backs. Or even to be overly concerned with what they would eat or wear. Now their priorities could be whatever the will of God was. In this case, Jesus said it would be "to catch men." They were going to learn by experience the principles of the Kingdom—principles that are still valid.

"Seek ye first the Kingdom of God and his righteousness," Jesus said, "and all these things shall be added unto you."[10]

Able To Forsake All

"And when they had brought their ships to land, they forsook all and followed him."[11]

So far this had been quite a day. Their ships were so heaped with fish they had to maneuver them to shore ever so carefully lest they should be swamped and sink. But there it was, the greatest single catch they had ever made; and in the shortest time. However, It wasn't the catch that astonished them; it was the man who had commanded it.

As Jesus stepped from the boat and made his way up the beach they followed him. There lay their boats, their nets, and the biggest catch of their lives. The scripture does not say that after they marketed their fish they followed Jesus. "Market" was no longer in their minds. That was for someone else now. They had tasted the kingdom of God where Jesus was Lord. Jesus had taught them a lesson they would never forget. Now they understood clearly, *what he commands he will bless*, whether it is fishing or preaching. Now they had a new philosophy and a new source of provision. The will of God for them was to catch men, not fish, because Jesus had called them.

Jesus was introducing them to truth that was in force before the fall. After the fall, Adam had lived as his offspring continued to live, by the sweat of his face. These men were well acquainted with that way. Work to survive was the only experience they had known until now. But in Jesus they were seeing God's life in a man: a life that was self-existent, with eternal and unlimited resources.

In Adam's case, God had made the environment, provided the sustenance and commissioned him to eat freely. Adam did not eat because he worked. He ate because God provided. With that established, God assigned him work, to dress and keep the garden.

Now Jesus had come. Although he had labored for many years as a carpenter, his work was not to sustain himself (that was the Father's responsibility) but to complete the task the Father had given him.[12] Peter and his partners were watching and learning. Soon they would be busier and working harder than ever before.

Jesus had worked faithfully at his trade until it was the Father's time to call him out. His calloused hands, no doubt, bore witness to his diligent labor as a carpenter. His disciples could see how tirelessly Jesus applied himself to his ministry now that God had called him from his shop. They could not have missed the lesson that God's blessing relates to every avenue of life whether it be carpentry, fishing, labor, business or preaching the gospel. It is the motivation that is important. Why do we do what we do? The motive must be to do the will of God. Our resources are not in what we can produce. They are in him.

The Will Of God Prevails.

"And it came to pass, when he was in a certain city, behold, a man full of leprosy: who, seeing Jesus fell on his face, and besought him, saying, 'Lord, if thou wilt, thou canst make me clean.' And he put forth his hand and touched him and said, 'I will, be thou clean.' And immediately the leprosy departed from him."[13]

Satan is the author of sin and death with all of its accoutrements. When he rules, bondage prevails. Although Jesus was in the world he was not governed by it. He was, in fact, the Kingdom of God personified. Where Jesus was, the will of God prevailed. The world was not in charge; JESUS, the man in whom God dwelt, was. When Jesus declared the cleansing of this particular leper to be the will of God, it was done.

Upon Jesus was placed the authority the first man had surrendered in the fall. His disciples, no doubt, stood in awe as they heard and saw the kingdom of God. This was preaching at its dynamic best. They were hearing and seeing God revealed in man.

Man Does What Only God Can Do

The Bible teaches us that in Christ dwells the fullness of the

Godhead, bodily.[14] Jesus is called the express image of the invisible God.[15] If one could see God, he would be exactly what we see in the person of Jesus Christ. Jesus, therefore, is the epitome of what humanity was created to be. It was no wonder, then, that:

"On a certain day as he was teaching, there were Pharisees and doctors of the law sitting by . . ., and the power of the Lord was present to heal [the sick.] And . . . men brought in a bed a man that was taken with the palsy: and they sought means to bring him in, and lay him before him. And when they could [find no way] because of the multitude, they went up onto the housetop, and let him down through the tiling. . . . And when Jesus saw their faith he said unto him, 'Man, thy sins be forgiven thee.'

The scribes and Pharisees began to reason saying, 'who is this that speaks blasphemies? Who can forgive sins but God alone?'

But when Jesus perceived their thoughts, he said, 'what reason ye in your hearts? Whether is easier to say, Thy sins be forgiven thee: or take up thy bed and walk? But that you may know that the Son of man hath power upon earth to forgive sins, (he said unto the sick of the palsy). I say unto you, arise, and take up thy couch, and go into your house.' And immediately he rose up. . . and departed to his own house glorifying God."[16]

Jesus was preaching the Kingdom of God. It is obvious that God reigns in that Kingdom. Jesus, doing God's will under God's authority had the authority of God. Jesus was perfect in holiness and wholly committed to doing what God was doing. No wonder, then, that Jesus, as a man, was doing what only God could do. The invisible God was made visible in the person of Jesus. God was in him to will and to do of his good pleasure.[17]

The Last Adam

Jesus' uniqueness was not in the fact that he was not human or that he was super human. Neither was the case. He was human. Furthermore, he himself declared his helplessness apart from the Father. He was the seed of a woman who was the offspring of Adam. Unlike other men who are spiritually dead from birth because of their father's sin nature, Jesus was alive in the Spirit from birth because of his Father's divine nature. Jesus was demonstrating the perfect human role.

But the work of God was more than producing enormous drafts of fish, more than physically healing victims of palsy and leprosy or feeding the multitudes, even more than raising the dead. It was the redemption of lost humanity.

This redemptive process required a spotless life, a perfect sacrifice. It required a man who had *chosen* to love the Father with all his heart, soul, mind and strength, and his neighbor as himself, a man who would willingly lay down his life as a ransom for lost humanity [18]and then take it up again to appear as their advocate before the Father.[19]

This man was The Word Of God who came forth from the bosom of the Father:

Being in the form of God, he thought it not robbery to be equal with God, but made himself of no reputation and took on him the form of a servant, and was made in the likeness of men: and being found in fashion as a man, he humbled himself, and became obedient unto death, even the death of the cross. Wherefore God hath given him a name that is above every name: that at the name of Jesus Christ every knee should bow, of things in heaven, and things in earth, and things under the earth; and that every tongue should confess that Jesus Christ is Lord to the glory of God the Father.[20]

Jesus demonstrated in his servitude, his obedience, and his humiliation the divine principle of the kingdom of God: those who exalt themselves will be abased. Even Lucifer who exalted himself, was cast down to the earth to be ultimately defeated by man. But those who humble themselves under the mighty hand of God, are ultimately exalted to sit with Christ in heavenly places, even as Jesus himself was exalted by the Father to be glorified at his right hand.

Unflagging confidence in God's promises, and submission to his revealed will assures dominion over the world, the flesh and the devil. That is the result of simple trust in the person of God, whatever our status or occupation.

Heaven's Authority

world's

authority

Jesus You

When you are saved, you are seated in heavenly places in/with Christ (Eph. 2:6). Now you, too, are in the world but not of it. Your citizenship and authority are in heaven. (Phil. 3:20)

CHAPTER 11 References
1. Luke 4:28–30
2. Luke 4:33–36
3. Luke 4:42
4. Luke 4:43
5. Luke 5:1–3
6. Luke 5:4–10
7. Genesis 3:19
8. II Thesselonians 3:6–10
9. Luke 4:4; Deuteronomy 8:3
10. Matthew 6:33
11. Luke 5:11
12. John 4:34; 17:4
13. Luke 5:12,13
14. Colossians 2:9
15. Colossians 1:15; Hebrews 1:3
16. Luke 5:17–25
17. Philippians 2:13
18. I Timothy 2:5,6
19. Hebrews 9:24
20. Philippians 2:6–11

Chapter 12
Renewing the Mind

The Lord Jesus Christ was born of God and of man at the same time. From his birth in Bethlehem to his death at Calvary, Jesus lived the life of the Spirit of God in his mortal body. Jesus, in the life he lived as a man, was our example. His was the normal Christian life. How is the average Christian different?

Our flesh is by nature corrupt through what the Bible describes as "deceitful lusts."[1] Even though we have been born again, our flesh has not been converted, nor will it be until we see Jesus.[2] When the Spirit of Christ becomes resident in our spirit, we are made children of God. From that moment on there is a contest between our flesh, and the Spirit within us. Paul wrote: *"The flesh lusteth against the Spirit, and the spirit against the flesh, and these are contrary the one to the other so that ye cannot do the things that ye would."*[3]

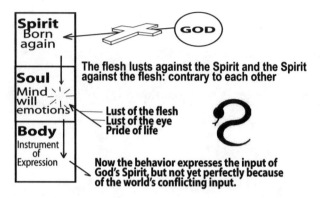

The flesh lusts against the Spirit and the Spirit against the flesh: contrary to each other

— Lust of the flesh
— Lust of the eye
— Pride of life

Now the behavior expresses the input of God's Spirit, but not yet perfectly because of the world's conflicting input.

Even though we are now alive in the Spirit, walking *after* the Spirit is not automatic. It is something we are commanded to do, and it is a satisfying exercise of faith and obedience.

In his unregenerate state, man is separated from the life of God by ignorance.[4] The natural man's knowledge of God is limited to religious precepts and doctrinal statements; in reality, however, he is ignorant of God. The New Testament states:

"The natural man receiveth not the things of the Spirit of God for they are foolishness unto him; neither can he know them because they are spiritually discerned."[5]

That same natural man, though, is well schooled in the philosophy of this world. The reader may be a good example of this. Being born again between the ages of 15 and 25 would place you among the average in that respect. You had a degree of maturity. Your world view, to a great degree, was formed. The world had already established, or at least greatly influenced, your good and evil value system, and possibly quite apart from any knowledge of what God has stated in his Word. If that is your case, you are typical of the natural man.

When this person is born again of the Spirit, although he immediately gains spiritual life, he does not suddenly develop a severe case of amnesia, thereby forgetting all he has learned from the world system. Nor does he acquire an instant education in spiritual truth. He is born, a spiritual infant, into the kingdom of God, and he is no less ignorant of the facts of the kingdom of God the moment after he is saved than he was the moment before.

True, he is now alive in Christ, delivered from the power of sin and death, and has gained citizenship in heaven. Beyond being aware of life, he is, as at his natural birth, helplessly ignorant. He must grow from infancy to spiritual maturity. If he remains ignorant, he will be separated from what there is for him in the life of God to a degree commensurate with his ignorance. We are instructed, therefore, to: *"Put off the old man which is corrupt through the deceitful lusts, and put on the new man which, after God is created in righteousness and true holiness.*[6]

Renewing the spirit of the mind[7] is a process of reeducation through spiritual discipline, Christian fellowship, and above all *The Word of God.* The apostle Peter commanded that as new born babes we should desire the sincere milk of the Word so that we can grow thereby.[8] Saturating ourselves in its truths, believing its precepts, and conforming to its principles, we mature in our knowledge of God and in our ability to overcome the unholy desires of the flesh. It is our response to God's Word that determines how much of God's revelation we understand. Jesus said, *"He that hath my commandments and keepeth them, he it is that loveth me: and he that loves me shall be loved of my Father, and I will love him and will manifest myself to him.'"*[9]

The bottom line is I *will manifest myself to him.* The prerequisite is *obedience*—having his commandments and keeping them.

Contemporary Christendom often places more emphasis on psychology, feelings, and amalgamative relationships than on the Word of God. Having God's commandments, therefore, and keeping them, is rather low on the priority list of many professing believers. What the Bible says about any given topic is simply another opinion, often considered inferior to the majority opinions of the day.

Obviously, those who share that evaluation of God's Word would find little incentive to search out its wisdom or instruction for their daily lives. They would, therefore, not be apt to *have* his commandments. Nor would it be likely, or even possible, that they would *keep* them.

In Psalm 119:128 it is written, "I esteem *all* thy precepts concerning *all* things to be right; and I hate every false way." Whoever this writer was, he had a predisposition to believe God about every subject. He was not critical of God's Word but receptive. No matter what the subject, God's view was correct. Thus he was not deceived by falsehood. He hated it.

Our view of God's Word determines our ability to obey it. And our willingness to search it out and obey it determines how much Jesus manifests himself to us. The apostle John wrote,

"When he (Jesus) shall appear we shall be like him for we shall see him as he is."[10].

We are waiting for an historic day in which Jesus shall appear and we will see him with our eyes. When we do, we shall be fully and finally conformed to his image. It is evident that seeing him as he is has something to do with that transformation.

There is a spiritual truth here that is applicable to the present time. A spiritual transformation can take place in us day by day as we "see him" with our spiritual understanding. The apostle Paul wrote, *"We. . . beholding the glory of the Lord are changed into the same image, from glory to glory."[11].*

The change in us is the result of beholding his glory. When we are obedient to his Word and he manifests himself to us, as he promised he would, we become like what we see him to be. And this is the point. We are to be growing up into the measure of the stature of the fullness of Christ.[12] That results, not from the mere accumulation of knowledge, but from a revelation of Him. That revelation is enhanced by our commitment to obey his Word.

The principle is well illustrated in the very beginning of history. We have discussed before how God had placed Adam in the garden of Eden and clearly defined his responsibilities. Every necessity was provided, including companionship with his wife and fellowship with God. Within the garden was the Tree of Life and the Tree of the knowledge of Good and Evil. God allowed Adam and his wife free access to the Tree of Life, but warned him that feeding upon the Tree of the knowledge of Good and Evil would dispel the idyllic environment of Eden and bring certain death to Adam and his seed.

The New Testament also makes a distinction between *knowledge* and *life*. In the natural world, *light* is equated with knowledge. The more knowledge we have of a subject, the more enlightened we say we are about it. In most cases that's fine, but the apostle Paul warns us of the danger of mere knowledge when applied to the kingdom of God. *"Knowledge puffeth up. . ."* he wrote.

John the apostle wrote, *"In him [Jesus] is life, and the life is the light of men."*[14]

Note that in this case, it is *life*, not knowledge, that is light. This is an important distinction that God wants us to understand. In the Garden of Eden the serpent promised enlightenment through the knowledge of good and evil. But that light did not bring life. In Adam's case it brought death.

When we are born into the kingdom of God through faith, it is imperative that we grow up through an ever increasing revelation of God. That increase does not come by simply multiplying knowledge. It is the result of Jesus manifesting himself to us. His *life* is our light. Paul said, *"Beholding his glory we are changed into his image."* In Christ is all knowledge, wisdom and understanding. As we put on the new man (the life of Christ), we are renewed in knowledge after the image of Christ who created us.[15]

At the time of our conversion we are already well acquainted with the philosophies of this world and its orientation to good and evil. From the time of our physical birth we have been bombarded with this world's values. Our personal value system has been developed by the influence of traditions, arts, education, religion, and every other social force that touches our lives. Thus we had a knowledge of good and evil, but it did not—could not— produce spiritual life.

In many of us the knowledge of good and evil didn't produce the slightest desire to do the good. Others of us who did desire to do good, didn't find the power to do it. Obviously, the knowledge of good and evil was not the key to a successful pursuit of righteous living.

When we come into Christ, our value system is carried over. We know God is good, so we understand instantly that he wants us to shun evil. Therefore, we respond by rejecting the evil that the world taught us, and we determine to govern our lives, from that point on, by what we think is good.

What we may not realize is that, as the world taught us what is evil, that same value system taught us our concept of what is good. If those values are not what God has revealed in his Word, what we discern to be good may have no resemblance to the will of God. Much conflict in the lives of believers exists because some of us are never weaned from our good and evil value system. As a consequence, much of our "rightness" is in contradiction to God's Word.[16] Our concern, then, is not simply what is good, but rather what is the will of God. Knowing good and evil is knowledge. Knowing God and doing his will is life.

Feeding at the Tree of Life, simply stated, means listening to the voice of God through his Word and by his Spirit. Those who both *have* and *keep* his Word are those that love him, and to them the Lord has promised to manifest himself. As the revelation of Christ increases, the Holy Spirit empowers us to abandon that which is of the old man and put on that which is of the new.[17]

"I beseech you, therefore, brethren, by the mercies of God, that ye present your bodies a living sacrifice, holy, acceptable unto God, which is your reasonable service. And be not conformed to this world; but be ye transformed by the renewing of your mind, that you may prove (demonstrate) what is that good, and acceptable, and perfect will of God."[18]

God's purpose for us in Christ is to demonstrate his will, as Adam did before the fall and as Jesus did. These men were the image of God. The body of Christ, the church, is the humanity in which God has now determined to demonstrate his personality, his attributes, and his works. Through it he has purposed to manifest his wisdom to the world and to the principalities and powers that have ruled over man from the time of Adam's disobedience until the resurrection of Jesus from the grave.[19]

It is incumbent upon believers to put off the old man, to put on the new, and to be renewed in the spirit of their mind. The story is told in the 11th chapter of John's gospel of Lazarus, whom Jesus raised from the dead. Lazarus' body had been anointed with great quantities of ointment, as was the custom, and bound up tightly with yards of material until he somewhat resembled a mummy. Then he had been laid in a tomb, and a great stone had been rolled against the opening to seal it up.

Four days later Jesus came on the scene. "Roll away the stone." he commanded. When they had complied, he stood before the open sepulchre and cried with a loud voice, "Lazarus, come forth."

Let's not miss the significance of this scene. There is no way Lazarus could have emerged under his own power from that grave. Even if he were alive, he could not have moved his arms or legs to remove himself from the stone shelf on which he lay. Had he been standing up, he could not have walked.

It was the power of Jesus' words alone that carried him out and placed him alive among his kinfolk. This is a picture of the power of grace that brought every one of us who are saved out of darkness into light and gave us life.

The next scene, also, is allegorical to our condition. Lazarus is standing, or lying, alive in front of his tomb. But he still very much resembles a dead man. He is still bound hand and foot with grave clothes. There is still work to be done before he is free. So Jesus commands, "Loose him, and let him go."

Many of God's people are still encumbered with the philosophies of the world that they carried with them out of the tomb. Their good and evil value system which they received from the Tree of the knowledge of Good and Evil still binds them hand and foot and covers their eyes as did the napkin that bound Lazarus' face. There is a need, therefore, to be renewed in the spirit of their mind.

In the 12th chapter of John, the follow-up of the story has Lazarus sitting at the table dining with Jesus, and all Jesus' enemies have become his enemies too. His fellowship with Jesus has obviously brought him into a new and different relationship with the world around him.

We learn from these New Testament scenes that there are steps beyond regeneration. There is the requirement to be loosed from all that we incurred when we were dead in sin. And then we need to seek a continually greater revelation of the Lord Jesus through fellowship with him in his word. The apostle Paul said it well when he said simply, "If we live in the Spirit, let us also walk in the Spirit."

CHAPTER 12 References
1. Ephesians 4:22
2. I Corinthians 15:51–54
3. Galatians 5:22
4. Ephesians 4:18
5. I Corinthians 2:14
6. Ephesians 4:22
7. Ephesians 4:23
8. I Peter 2:2,3
9. John 14:21
10. I John 3:2
11. II Corinthians 3:18
12. Ephesians 4:13,14
13. I Corinthians 8:1
14. John 1:4
15. Colossians 3:10
16. Isaiah 64:6
17. Ephesians 4:22,24
18. Romans 12:1,2
19. Ephesians 3:10

Chapter 13
Christ in His Whole Church

Some may assume that if we may live this present life by the principles Jesus lived by, each of us can, and even should be another Jesus. If Christ is in us we should be doing all that he did, and being all that he was. That thinking is responsible for much confusion among Christians. In trying to imitate Jesus' life, they fail. Failure produces discouragement, so they give up and try to return to the world. Perhaps this is what happened to Curtis (see chapter 1), and has happened to others like him.

But we are not Jesus, nor are we to imitate him. We are a corporate vessel in which the Holy Spirit does a genuine and original work. Jesus is at work in the whole body, which is made up of many members. Collectively, the believers are what he was alone, *The Body of Christ.* In this age Jesus is the head. We, the Church, are the body.[1]

"For as the body is one, and hath many members, and all the members of that one body being many, are one body: so also is Christ. For by one Spirit are we all baptized into one body, whether we be bond or free: and have been all made to drink into one Spirit. For the body is not one member, but many."[2]

God has taken us who were dead in trespasses and sin, without

121

any capacity for righteousness, and has baptized us by his Holy Spirit into the body of his Son.[3] By that one act we have literally become members of the body in which God dwells and walks.[4] We are the visible humanity in which God will express himself now and for eternity. In the kingdom of heaven, we are no more strangers and foreigners but fellow citizens, members of the household of God.[5]

In Adam's race, every member was a part of the first man, bearing his image, manifesting his nature. Now, in the new creation, every member is a part of the second man, Christ. Jesus is the head of a new species of man, and all the members together are the body. Collectively, they become one living testimony of the person of God.

When the apostle Paul told the Philippian believers, "It is God that worketh in you both to will and to do of his good pleasure,"[6] he was speaking to the collective fellowship of believers in that city. As each one obeys the leading of the Holy Spirit,[7] the whole body performs the will of God.

Obviously, as God perfects the whole body, he is perfecting the individuals in it. But no individual member will be perfect before the whole body is perfect, and the whole body cannot be perfect without all of its members.

You Are Important

This is the reason Paul said to the Roman believers, *"I beseech you brethren. . .that you present your bodies (*plural*) a living sacrifice* (singular*), holy, acceptable unto God, which is your reasonable service."*[8]

Speaking naturally, it's the behavior of your body that lets others know what is going on in your spirit. That is true spiritually as well. Unless the body is submitted to the Spirit of God, it is not available to demonstrate his will.

Our example is the Lord Jesus. He was "The Lamb of God"[9] set apart to do only the will of him that sent him. From birth until death, he was a living sacrifice, separated and marked for death.[10] At the cross he became the offering for sin. The living sacrifice was slain.

During those years of his life in which he was the living sacrifice, his body was the humanity in which men saw God. His actions, his character, and his words were directed by the Father who dwelt in him.[11] Now, those who are in Christ are that Body. It is in *their* humanity that the work and wisdom of God are to be manifest.

"And be not conformed to this world, but be ye transformed by the renewing of your mind, that you may prove (demonstrate) what is that good, and acceptable, and perfect will of God."[8]

In no way was Jesus conformed to this world. He knew the world was dead in trespasses and sin, captive to the devil, and at enmity with God. Conforming to the world would be totally incompatible with being sacrificed to the Father's will. He was not motivated by lust for fame or financial gain. He was completely available for the Father to do in him whatever he would. It was God, therefore, that worked in Him.[11]

Christ's Inheritance In The Saints

Paul prayed for the Ephesian church that the eyes of their understanding would be enlightened, that they would know what is Christ's inheritance in the saints.[12] *Our* inheritance in *him* would include such things as eternal life, a heavenly hope, physical resurrection, eternal perfection, etc. But how are we to understand *his* inheritance in *us*? What would that include? If, indeed, he has an inheritance in us, there is the implication that we are of eternal value to him.

When Jesus was on earth his flesh was the body of Christ. But after his resurrection he ascended to the Father as the head of the body of Christ.[13] If, somehow, a head could be severed from its body without impairing its thought processes, it could not implement any action. That, in a sense, was the dilemma of Adam without Eve. He knew the commission of God, to multiply and fill the earth, but he could not fulfill it without his bride. He was a head without a body.

So it is with Jesus. In the church, he has inherited not only a future bride (that is the joy that is set before him),[14] but a present body through which he has ordained the implementation of his will in the earth. The Father expressed himself and demonstrated his will through the humanity of Jesus (in him dwells the fullness of the godhead bodily).[15] Now the church, made up of all the redeemed, is the body of humanity through which Christ expresses himself and implements the doing of the Father's will. (it is God that worketh in you both to will and to do of his good pleasure).[16] The saints who are the body of Christ are his inheritance.[17] It is through them that the will of the head is carried out in the earth.

As those who make up that body yield their members as instruments of righteousness unto God,[18] he exercises his various gifts and ministries in them as he wills.[19] In this way he coordinates the work of the whole church to reveal himself and to fulfill his own purposes in the earth. When that work is done, then he will put in place the final step, the redemption of the body.[20]

The Finale

We have already commented on the resurrection of Jesus. We have seen what a thrilling reality that was. It became the very center of the Gospel. A man had conquered death. Now he lives forever without the potential ever to die again.[21] That glorious truth has provoked more hope, more praise, more hallelujahs than any other fact of history. Even so, the Bible describes that event as only the firstfruits.[22]

How glorious the day will be when the harvest comes, and the whole crop is gathered together. Then we will experience eternally and perfectly what is meant by: *"As we have borne the image of the earthly, we shall bear also the image of the heavenly."[23]*

That will be the redemption of the body. The conflict between the flesh and the spirit will be over. Physically, there will be no more pain, sorrow or dying.[24] Even the potential of sin and death will be done away.

Paul probably had a smile on his face and a shout of glory in his heart when he wrote:

"Behold, I show you a mystery; we shall not all sleep, but we shall all be changed: in a moment, in the twinkling of an eye, at the last trump: for the trumpet shall sound, and the dead shall be raised incorruptible, and we shall be changed. For this corruptible must put on incorruption, and this mortal shall put on immortality. So when this corruptible shall have put on incorruption, and this

mortal shall have put on immortality, then shall be brought to pass the saying that is written, death is swallowed up in victory. "[25]

It is then that God's eternal purpose, "*let us make man in our image*" will be realized.

The first man was mortal, with the potential of sin and death. He was in fellowship with God without choice or recourse. When the option was presented, the man chose sin and died. The redeemed in Christ are *willingly* in fellowship with God, placed there by God's incomparable grace, through the righteous obedience of the Lord Jesus Christ. They, too, are ultimately to be made immortal, without the potential of sin or death, to exist truly and eternally in the image of God. Then comes the beginning.

I say the *beginning* because all that has happened in time, from the creation of the world to the last trumpet when the dead shall be raised incorruptible, has been the temporal process of creating man and conforming him to the image of Christ. All of this has been preliminary to God's eternal purpose. When that great resurrection is passed and God's temporal program is finished, when we stand in our immortal and incorruptible bodies conformed absolutely to the image of Christ, God will say, "There, I have finished Genesis 1:26. I have made man in the image of God."

Then that redeemed humanity, the Body of Christ, will be the express and visible image of the invisible God for all eternity. That will be the Body in and through which God will work and manifest himself throughout the eternal ages.

How often I have wondered and how often I have been asked, "But what will it be like? What will we be doing?" The answer is always the same:

"Eye hath not seen, nor ear heard, nor hath entered into the heart of man the things that God hath prepared for them that love him. But God hath revealed them unto us by his Spirit."[26] **"Now we see through a glass darkly, but then, face to face."[27]**

The Beginning

125

CHAPTER 13 References
1. Ephesians 1:22,23
2. I Corinthians 12:12-14
3. I Corinthians 12:13
4. II Corinthians 6:16
5. Ephesians 2:19
6. Philippians 2:13
7. Romans 8:14
8. Romans 12:1,2
9. John 1:29,36
10. Hebrews 2:9
11. John 14:9
12. Ephesians 1:18
13. Hebrews 12:2
14. Colossians 2:9
15. Philippians 2:13
16. Romans 6:13
17. I Corinthians 12:4-11
18. Romans 8:23;Ephesians 1:14
19. Romans 6:9
20. I Corinthians 15:20-23
21. I Corinthians 15:48-49
22. Revelation 21:4
23. I Corinthians 15:51-54
24. I Corinthians 2:4,10
25. I Corinthians 13:12

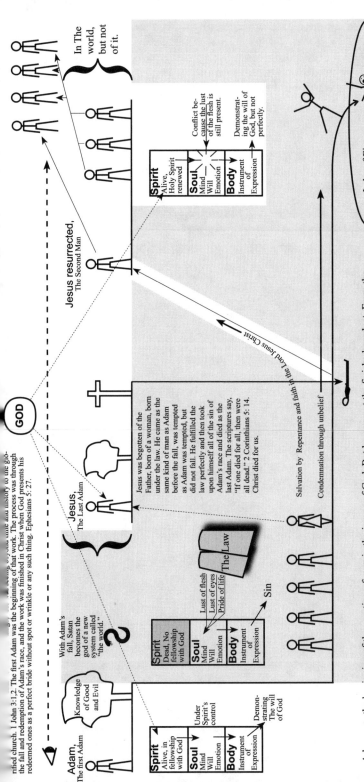

Adam was the beginning of the creation of man in the image of God. But he was not the finished product. From the beginning he had the potential of sin and death (PSD). When Adam exercised his will, and chose to disobey God, he died spiritually and was no longer in fellowship with God. All of his offspring were born in this condemnation. Jesus Identified with them in his death. Now they have the option to identify with him in his resurrection by repentance toward God and faith in the finished work of Christ on their behalf. Those who belive receive eternal life in Christ; those who do not continue in condemnation. Now those who are in Christ are saved, but they still contend with the flesh while they wait for the resurrection and the redemption of their bodies. Romans 8: 23. Meanwhile, the church is in heaven and in earth.

rified church. 1 John 3:1,2. The first Adam was the beginning of that work. The process was through the fall and redemption of Adam's race, and the work was finished in Christ when God presents his redeemed ones as a perfect bride without spot or wrinkle or any such thing. Ephesians 5: 27.